The Intrinsic View of the Body of Christ

Witness Lee

Living Stream Ministry
Anaheim, CA • www.lsm.org

First Edition, December 1991.

ISBN 978-0-87083-636-7

Published by

Living Stream Ministry
2431 W. La Palma Ave., Anaheim, CA 92801 U.S.A.
P. O. Box 2121, Anaheim, CA 92814 U.S.A.

Printed in the United States of America

11 12 13 14 15 16 / 11 10 9 8 7 6 5

CONTENTS

PREFACE

This book is composed of messages given by Brother Witness Lee in Reston, Virginia on November 28—December 1, 1991.

CHAPTER ONE

THE ISSUE OF GOD'S IMPARTATION AND TRANSMISSION IN HIS DIVINE TRINITY INTO HIS CHOSEN PEOPLE, AS THE CHURCH THE FULLNESS OF THE ONE WHO FILLS ALL IN ALL

Scripture Reading: Eph. 1:3-6, 7-12, 13-14, 18-23

OUTLINE

I. The issue of God the Father's impartation:
  A. Of His holy nature into His chosen people that they may be separated from the world and sanctified wholly unto Him—Eph. 1:4.
  B. Of His divine life into His predestinated people that they may become His many sons for His expression—v. 5.
  C. To the praise of the glory (expression) of His grace—v. 6.

II. The issue of God the Son's impartation of the divine element into God the Father's chosen and predestinated people:
  A. In the redemption through His blood—v. 7.
  B. To bring them into Christ as their sphere and element, that they may be made God's inheritance, with the divine element in Christ, as a treasure to God—vv. 8-11.
  C. To the praise of God the Father's glory (expression) in the believers who have first hoped in Christ—v. 12.

III. The issue of God the Spirit's impartation of the divine
essence into God the Father's inheritance redeemed
by God the Son:
  A. By sealing it (God's inheritance) that it may be
     saturated with the divine essence as the impress
     to be a mark and the image of God to be His
     expression—v. 13.
  B. By being a pledge of God as His redeemed people's
     inheritance for their foretaste of Him, guarantee-
     ing their full taste of Him, unto the redemption of
     His acquired possession (redeemed inheritance)—
     v. 14a.
  C. To the praise of God's glory (expression)—v. 14b.
IV. The issue of the transmission of God in His divine
trinity into His chosen and redeemed people:
  A. As the great power toward the believers, which
     God caused to operate in Christ:
     1. In raising Him from the dead.
     2. In seating Him at the Father's right hand in
        the heavenlies, far above all.
     3. In subjecting all things under His feet.
     4. In giving Him to be the Head over all things.
  B. As the transmission to the church, which is the
     Body of Christ, the One who fills all in all—
     vv. 19-23.

Prayer: Lord, we worship You that You are still moving on this earth. How we thank You that Your moving is going on among us in Your recovery. We remind You that whenever we come together into Your name, there is an oracle ready for You to speak to us. Lord, we are here opening to You. Come, Lord Jesus. Speak to us. We want to hear, and we want to listen to Your word. Lord Jesus, we have no trust in ourselves. We put our trust in You, in Your mercy, in Your blessing, in Your presence, in Your anointing, and in Your reaching each one of us. We consecrate and offer this conference to You. Even tonight we present this meeting to You as a burnt offering. Lord, visit each one of us. We want to be touched by You that we may touch You. Sanctify these four days of this conference. Sanctify all of us wholly unto You. We are here not for our interest but for Your interest, especially in these last days as You are moving on this earth to cut short Your word, to accomplish Your prophecy and Your promises. Lord Jesus, we want to be fully for You. Gain us, possess us, occupy us, and use us. Lord Jesus, we thank You for Yourself. We thank You for what You are. Defeat the enemy. We accuse him in front of You. We are touching Your throne of authority. O Lord Jesus, put Your enemy to the corner. Do something further and further and further until You arrive at Your goal. Thank You, Lord Jesus, in Your mighty name.

THE BODY OF CHRIST IN EPHESIANS

The burden of these messages concerning the Body of Christ can be expressed in the following four statements:

1) The Body of Christ is the fullness of the One who fills all in all—Eph. 1:23.

2) Christ created the two, Jews and Gentiles, in Himself into one new man as the poem of God, that God might display the surpassing riches of His grace toward us in Christ—Eph. 2:15, 10, 7.

3) To be strengthened into the inner man, that Christ may make His home in our hearts, that we may be filled unto all the fullness of God—Eph. 3:16-17, 19.

4) One Body, one Spirit, one Lord, one God, an indivisible

mingling of the Triune God with the believers in Christ—
Eph. 4:4-6, 12-16.

Our burden for this conference is on the Body of Christ.
The book of Ephesians is not merely concerning the church.
It is a book on the church as the Body of Christ. No other book
of the New Testament refers to the Body of Christ as much
as Ephesians does. Ephesians 1 says that the church is the
Body of Christ, the fullness of the One who fills all in all
(vv. 22-23). Chapter two says that Christ created the two, the
Jewish and Gentile believers, into one new man that He
might reconcile both in one Body to God (vv. 15-16). What a
mystery and what a gospel this is! Even our reconciliation
to God is not an individual matter. It is corporate. All the
believers have been reconciled to God in one Body. Chapter
three tells us that in Christ Jesus the saved Gentiles and the
saved Jews are fellow members of the Body (v. 6) and that this
Body is the fullness of God (v. 19) for the ultimate corporate
expression of the consummated Triune God. Chapter four
speaks of one Body, one Spirit, one Lord, one God and Father,
(vv. 4-6) and of all the saints needing to be perfected that they
may be able to do the work of the New Testament ministry to
build up the Body of Christ (vv. 11-12). This chapter also says
that out from the Head, Christ, all the Body grows by the
members growing so that the Body can be built up by itself
through all the functioning members in love (v. 16). This is
the Body of Christ in Ephesians.

THE ORGANIC BODY OF CHRIST

In order to see the revelation of the Body of Christ, it is
helpful to consider our physical body. My body is not a lifeless
organization but a living organism. When I speak, my entire
body participates in my speaking in a living and organic way.
The Body of Christ is an organism. An organism is something
of life. If there is no life, there is no organism. Christ's Body
is organic. It is a matter of life.

Now we need to consider the life with which the Body of
Christ is constituted. According to Genesis 1 and 2, in the
whole universe created by God there are lives on four levels.
Firstly, there is the plant life, the lowest level of life (1:11-12).

The next level of life is the animal life (vv. 20-25). Then Genesis shows us the third level of life, which is the human life (vv. 26-27). This is a life that is not God's life, but a life that can be like God. As the created people, we did not have God's life. God did not put His life into man when He created him. But God did create us with a life that resembles Him. This is similar to a photo of a person. It does not have the person's life, but it does bear his image. In a sense, the photo of a person is that person, but in an actual sense, it is not that person. We have to realize that in Genesis 1 God created man in His image as a photo of Himself. Genesis also shows us a life higher than the human life. This is the fourth level of life, the highest level of life, the life of the tree of life (2:9). This life is the life of God, the divine life. Thus, Genesis 1 and 2 reveal the plant life, the animal life, the human life, and the divine life.

The Body of Christ is altogether organic. It is a matter of life, but of what life? Surely the Body of Christ is not of the plant life or of the animal life. Then is it of the human life or of the divine life? Actually, the life of the Body of Christ is a mingled life, a life that is a mingling of God's life and man's life. The model of such a mingled life can be seen in the four Gospels. The four Gospels are four biographies of one person—Jesus Christ. The four Gospels show us a person who is both God and man. He was God but He was also a little child in a manger. How could God in the heavens, who is so majestic, great, marvelous, and glorious come to be in a manger? Who was that little child lying in a manger by the name of Jesus? He was a God-child. He had bones, flesh, and blood. He was a real boy, but He was also God.

When He grew up to be thirty years of age, He came out to minister. When people saw the things He did, they wondered who He was. Some said, "Is not this the carpenter, the son of Mary, and the brother of James and Joses and Judas and Simon? And are not His sisters here with us?" (Mark 6:3). Who was this One? This One was not merely a man. He was God *plus* man. "In the beginning was the Word, and the Word was with God, and the Word was God" (John 1:1). This Word, who was God, became flesh (v. 14).

Four thousand years after Adam was created and about two thousand years ago, God became flesh. According to God's reckoning, this was just two days ago since to Him a thousand years is as one day (2 Pet. 3:8). Thus, we can say that He became flesh the day before yesterday. The very God in eternity became a lowly man in time! He is the complete God plus the perfect man by the name of Jesus. *Jesus* means Jehovah the Savior. Who is Jesus? He is Jehovah the Savior; the very infinite God in eternity became our Savior. In order for Him to become the Savior of us sinners, He needed to become a man. He needed a human body and blood to shed for our sins.

Now there is such a unique One in the universe who is both God and man. He is God plus man. He lived on earth for thirty-three and a half years. Then He went voluntarily to the cross and died there for us. Hebrews 9:14 indicates that when He went to the cross to offer Himself to God, He was not alone because the Holy Spirit was with Him to strengthen Him. His offering of Himself to God as a sacrifice was strengthened by the third of the Divine Trinity. When He was hanging on the cross, the Father, the first of the Divine Trinity, was also with Him. His death was not merely the death of a man. His death was the death of God plus man.

The Lord was crucified from the third hour, 9:00 a.m. (Mark 15:25), to the ninth hour, 3:00 p.m. He suffered on the cross for six hours. At 12:00 noon, the sixth hour, darkness fell over all the land until the ninth hour (Matt. 27:45). For the first three hours, from 9:00 a.m. to 12:00 noon, He was persecuted by men for doing God's will; in the last three hours, He was judged by God to accomplish our redemption. It was during this time that God counted Him as our Substitute who suffered for our sin (Isa. 53:10). Darkness fell over all the land because our sin and sins and all negative things were being dealt with there; and because of our sin, God forsook Him (Matt. 27:46). God put all the sin of the world upon Him (Isa. 53:6), making Him sin on our behalf (2 Cor. 5:21). He died on the cross under God's judgment. He cried out, "My God, My God, why have You forsaken Me?" (Matt. 27:46). God forsook Him for our sake and for the sake of our sins. God forsook Christ on the cross because He took the place of sinners (1 Pet. 3:18). He bore our sins (2:24; Isa. 53:6) and was made sin for us (2 Cor. 5:21). In the three hours from 12:00 noon to 3:00 p.m., He was condemned by God, judged by God, and cut off by God from the land of the living for our sake.

Then He was buried, and after three days He rose up out of death. When He rose from among the dead, He did not drop His humanity. To say that Christ is no longer human after His resurrection is absolutely wrong and heretical. On the day of His resurrection in the evening, He came back to His disciples. Although the doors were shut where the disciples were, He appeared in their midst and said to them "Peace to you" (Luke 24:36). His disciples became frightened and thought they beheld a ghost (v. 37 and note 37[1]—Recovery Version). Then He said, "See My hands and My feet, that it is I Myself. Touch Me and see, for a spirit does not have flesh and bones as you behold Me having" (v. 39). Although He was resurrected, He was a man with a physical body that could be touched.

When He appeared in the midst of His disciples, He did not speak much to them. Instead, He breathed into them and said to them, "Receive the Holy Spirit" (John 20:22). The Holy Spirit is the holy *pneuma,* the holy breath. The Lord breathed Himself into them as the holy breath. A person's breath is actually himself. The Spirit breathed into the disciples is Christ. First Corinthians 15:45b says that the last Adam, Christ, became a life-giving Spirit. This Spirit, who is the Spirit of Jesus, is a Spirit with humanity. No one can fully comprehend this divine mystery.

There is a brother among us who is a professor of physics at the University of California at Berkeley. I recently asked him whether the very Christ who was standing in the midst of the disciples on the day of resurrection was physical or spiritual. He said that he did not know. This is a mystery which no one can understand. Today the very Christ in resurrection still has the human nature. Even in His resurrection and in His ascension, He is both divine and human. Is this not wonderful? The life-giving Spirit of Christ is not merely the Spirit of God. Now He is the compounded Spirit. He is compounded with divinity, plus humanity, plus the wonderful all-inclusive death of Christ and the powerful resurrection of Christ. This is the consummated Spirit who is the very consummation of the Triune God.

Today when someone believes in the Lord Jesus, he receives the consummated Spirit of life as the eternal life. The eternal life is a mingled life—a life of divinity mingled with humanity. The Lord Jesus said that He is the eternal life (John 14:6a), and by believing into Him, we received Him as the all-inclusive life-giving Spirit. In Him we have the complete God and the perfect man. In Him we can also participate in His all-inclusive death. His death is a dear death. We all have to love this death, to "kiss" this death. His death is different from the death of Adam. The death of Adam is terrible, but the death of Christ is wonderful. In Him we also have the powerful resurrection. Thus, in Him we have God—complete, man—perfect, death—all-inclusive, and resurrection—powerful, compounded together as one. This is the life we received when we believed in the Lord Jesus. This is clearly revealed in the New Testament, but not many realize that the eternal life which they have received is such a mingled life. The Body of Christ is of such a life. We may talk much about the Body of Christ, but I am concerned that we may not realize that this Body is of such a wonderful life. We all have to see this.

Now we may ask how such a life could get into us. This is why we have to read Ephesians. Ephesians 1 is a particular, skillfully written chapter telling us how this wonderful life has gotten into us. We may have read Ephesians 1 many times without seeing this. This is why, in chapter one of Ephesians, Paul prayed that God would give us a spirit of wisdom and revelation (v. 17). Paul prayed that God would open up our eyes, giving us the ability to know the wonderful, mysterious things recorded in Ephesians. We may read Ephesians 1 without a spirit of wisdom and revelation, without the opening of our inner eyes. Thus, we do not have the ability to apprehend the divine things. I have been praying much for all of us since the day we decided to have this conference. I desired that the Lord would grant us a spirit of wisdom and revelation to see Ephesians 1. This chapter is a deep mine. I want to open up this mine and show us the treasures in this mine.

THE BODY OF CHRIST BEING THE ISSUE OF GOD'S IMPARTATION AND TRANSMISSION IN HIS DIVINE TRINITY

The title of this first chapter says that the Body of Christ is the issue of God's impartation and transmission. If you are going to know the Body of Christ, you have to know God's impartation and God's transmission. The issue, the coming out, of God's impartation and transmission is the Body of Christ. This divine impartation and divine transmission is in His divine trinity. God was imparted to us and transmitted to us in His divine trinity. When I came up to the platform to speak this evening, I did not jump up. I took three steps to get to the platform. God is imparted and transmitted to us in His divine trinity in three steps, or stages.

John 3:16 is a familiar verse to us. It says that God so loved the world that He gave His only begotten Son. Sometimes I asked why this verse did not say that He sent His only begotten Son to us. But it says that He gave His only begotten Son to us. How did God give His Son? He could not give His Son in a simple way. He gave His Son in His divine trinity. God imparted Himself into us and transmitted all that He is into us in His divine trinity—in the Father, in the Son, and in the Spirit.

He imparts and transmits Himself into His chosen people. We are not merely people created by God. We have also been chosen by Him. We may not feel that we have been chosen by God, but Ephesians 1:4 says that before the foundation of the world, God chose us, selected us. He chose us to impart and transmit Himself into us. We are His divine chosen people as the church, and the church is the fullness of the One who fills all in all (vv. 22-23).

Actually ten messages are needed to convey the burden embodied in the title of this first chapter—"The Issue of God's Impartation and Transmission in His Divine Trinity into His

Chosen People, as the Church, the Fullness of the One Who Fills All in All." We need many messages for a full definition of this subject. We trust, however, that the Lord's burden can be released in our short word here. We need to keep in mind that God imparted Himself into us in His trinity—first in the Father, second in the Son, and third in the Spirit.

THE ISSUE OF GOD THE FATHER'S IMPARTATION

The church is the issue of God the Father's impartation of His holy nature into His chosen people that they may be separated from the world and sanctified wholly unto Him. Ephesians 1:4 says that before the foundation of the world, God chose us to be holy. God's choosing has a goal—to make us holy. The Chinese have their notion about what it is to be holy. They say that Confucius was holy. This, however, is not the biblical notion of what it means to be holy. The Bible reveals that in the whole universe, only One is holy; that One is God Himself. Besides God everything is common, unholy. Then how could we common people be made holy? How could a common American be made holy, since in the whole universe only One is holy—God? Let us use gold as an illustration. Gold signifies God in His divine nature. Only gold is golden. No other metal is golden. We are like black iron. How can black iron become golden? God can make us holy only by one way. He must impart Himself, especially His holy nature, into our being. We are a piece of iron, but gold has been added and inserted into our being. Thus, we are "golden iron."

If I were to ask you whether you are holy, you probably would not have the boldness to say so because of your poor condition. We need to see what it means to be holy. Only God is holy, so to be holy means to have God in you. Do you have God in you? A brother has God in him, but why does he still quarrel with his wife? This is because he has too much "iron." He forgot that he has at least a small amount of gold. We often forget that we have gold in us.

How can God make us holy? He makes us holy by imparting His holy nature into us. Before we were born, before the foundation of the world, God chose us to be holy. Before the foundation of the world, He imparted Himself into us as the holy nature. We may not be able to see how God could have imparted His holy nature into us before the foundation of the world. To help us see this, I would like to ask when we were regenerated. First Peter 1:3 tells us that God regenerated us through the resurrection of Christ. When Christ was resurrected, we were regenerated. This is God's way to reckon time. We all were made holy before the foundation of the world. It was then that God imparted Himself as the holy nature into our being.

God the Father also predestinated us that we may become His sons (Eph. 1:5). How could we become His sons? There is no other way but by God's imparting Himself as life into us. The church is the issue of God the Father's impartation of His divine life into His predestinated people that they may become His many sons for His expression. God imparted His divine life into us, so we were born as sons of God. By His choosing He imparted His holy nature into us, and by His predestinating He imparted His divine life into us. His holy nature makes us holy, and His divine life makes us sons of God. God's predestinating us unto sonship is for the praise of the glory of His grace, that is, for the praise of His expression in grace (v. 6).

Are we holy? We have to be bold to say, "Yes." Are we sons of God? We have to say, "Amen." This is because we have the holy nature of God in us and the divine life in us. The realization that we have God's holy nature and divine life should cause us to rejoice. We are holy, and we are the sons of God. This is because of the impartation of God the Father.

THE ISSUE OF GOD THE SON'S IMPARTATION OF THE DIVINE ELEMENT INTO GOD THE FATHER'S CHOSEN AND PREDESTINATED PEOPLE

The church is also the issue of God the Son's impartation of the divine element into God the Father's chosen and predestinated people (Eph. 1:7-12). God the Son redeemed us through His blood (v. 7). If we had not been lost, we would not have needed to be redeemed. Before we were saved, we were in Adam, in the world, in sin, and in death. But Christ came, and He redeemed us out of Adam into Himself, out of the world into Himself, out of sin into Himself, and out of death into Himself. We are now in Him. In the New Testament there is such a big phrase—*in Him*. We all need to say, "Hallelujah for *in Him*." We need to realize where we are right now. We are in Christ, the second of the Divine Trinity, the Son of God who is the very embodiment of the Father. We have been redeemed by Him into Him.

How marvelous it is that we are in Christ! Christ has become our sphere, our realm, and our element. The Father's nature and life are the substance, and the Son's element is the content of the divine nature and life. In the human nature and in the human life, there is the human element. Now since we have the divine nature and the divine life, we have the divine element. In this element and with this element, God made us a new creation (2 Cor. 5:17). This new creation is a precious treasure to God.

We have been brought into Christ as our sphere and element that we may be made God's inheritance with the divine element in Christ, as a treasure to God (Eph. 1:8-11). This treasure becomes God's inheritance. If we were still in Adam, in the world, in sin, and in death, God would not take us as His inheritance. How could we be sinners, yet become God's inheritance? We have become His inheritance by being put into Christ. In Christ and with Christ, we all have been created as a new creation, and this new creation is God's possession. God's possession is God's inheritance.

God treasures us. In God's eyes, we are no longer sinners. We are like a diamond to Him. God treasures us as His possession, His inheritance, in Christ. In Christ God can have all created things headed up into one (v. 10). Today we all have Christ, and we all are in Christ. Hallelujah, we are one! In the world there is no oneness. In the church, all the races are represented. We have people among us who are white, black, yellow, brown, and red, but all of us are one in Christ. We all are headed up into one in Christ. Since Christ has redeemed us into Himself as the element, He has imparted His element, the divine element, into our being. We have not only the divine nature and life but also the element of this nature and life. This is the impartation of God the Son in the second person of the Divine Trinity.

THE ISSUE OF GOD THE SPIRIT'S IMPARTATION OF THE DIVINE ESSENCE INTO GOD THE FATHER'S INHERITANCE REDEEMED BY GOD THE SON

The church as the Body of Christ is the issue of God the Spirit's impartation of the divine essence into God the Father's inheritance redeemed by God the Son. Following the redemption of the Son, the Spirit of God comes to seal us (Eph. 1:13). When someone buys a book, he may put his seal upon it to indicate that the book is his. The seal has the sealing ink. When you put the seal upon a piece of paper, the sealing ink saturates and permeates the paper. To saturate is something vertical, and to permeate is something horizontal. Because we have been redeemed into Christ, Christ is the element in which we have been made God's treasure, God's inheritance, God's possession. Since we are God's inheritance, He put His Holy Spirit into us as a seal to mark us out, indicating that we belong to Him. God put a mark on us, and this mark, this seal, is the inking, saturating, and permeating Spirit.

While the word is being ministered in the meetings, the sealing Spirit is saturating us vertically and permeating us horizontally to make us full of the imparting God. When a brother returns home after attending a weekend conference, his relatives may say that he is different. He is different because in the conference he was permeated, saturated, and sealed thoroughly with the Spirit for the entire weekend. This sealing produces a mark to indicate ownership. The seal also impresses its image on the object being sealed. The sealing of the Spirit causes us to bear the image of God.

The sealing of the Spirit, the saturating and permeating of the Spirit, takes place continually in us. This sealing will go on until the redemption of our body, the transfiguration of our body (1:14; 4:30). Today the sealing within us is going on vertically and horizontally to transform and transfigure us. As God's inheritance, we are sealed that we may be saturated with the divine essence as the impress to be a mark and the image of God to be His expression.

While this sealing Spirit is saturating us, He remains with us as a pledge (1:14). This pledge is a guarantee that God will be our inheritance. The Spirit as the pledge of our inheritance is a foretaste of what we shall inherit of God, affording us a taste beforehand of the full inheritance. The Lord within us can be tasted, and His taste is sweet, pleasant, and good (1 Pet. 2:3; Psa. 34:8), but this is just a foretaste. The full taste is coming. When we are enjoying the foretaste, we realize this foretaste guarantees that God is coming to be our full taste. The Spirit as the pledge of God as His redeemed people's inheritance for their foretaste of Him, guarantees their full taste of Him, unto the redemption of His acquired possession, His redeemed inheritance. This is to the praise of God's glory, God's expression (Eph. 1:14).

Thus far, we have seen that the Father's nature is imparted into us, the Father's life is imparted into us, the Son's element is imparted into us, and the Spirit's essence is also imparted into us. The essence is finer and more intrinsic than the element. In the substance there is the element, and in the element there is the essence. Now the Triune God as the substance, as the element, and as the essence are altogether imparted into us, and this imparting is still going on. This imparting is the dispensing.

Many in Christianity think that the Bible merely teaches people what to do and what not to do. This, however, is similar to the teachings of Confucius. Christ's salvation is not mainly to teach us but mainly to dispense Himself into us. This is why we need to call on the name of the Lord early in the morning, saying "O Lord Jesus." If some of you have never done this, I would encourage you to try it from today. In the morning the first thing you should do is to call on the name of the Lord three to eight times. In order not to bother others early in the morning, you can call "O Lord Jesus" softly. By practicing this, you will be a different person. By calling on the Lord, you receive the fresh dispensing.

We can also receive the divine dispensing by praying over two or three verses from the holy Word each morning.

Perhaps we would open to John 1:1 and pray, "In the beginning was the Word. Lord Jesus You are in the beginning. You are the Word." We can pray-read this verse and another verse for about ten minutes. Then we will be refreshed because we have received the fresh dispensing.

During the day whenever we become tired, we should call, "O Lord Jesus." Much of the time my work is mainly to write and compose at my desk. Quite often I become tired out. Then when I say "O Lord Jesus" for a few minutes, I am refreshed. This is the way to receive the Triune God, to receive His dispensing, to receive His divine impartation and transmission.

The church is the issue of the divine impartation and the divine transmission of God the Father's nature and life, of God the Son's element, and of God the Spirit's essence. Nothing can exceed this threefold impartation. This impartation is more than mere teaching. Some people may say that I am a Bible teacher. That is not bad, but I am not satisfied with this. I want to be a person who always gives others a divine "shot," a divine injection. When I minister the word, I want to give people an injection of the Triune God, which is His impartation and transmission.

THE ISSUE OF THE TRANSMISSION
OF GOD IN HIS DIVINE TRINITY
INTO HIS CHOSEN AND REDEEMED PEOPLE

The final section of Ephesians 1 reveals that the church as the Body of Christ is the issue of the transmission of God in His divine trinity into His chosen and redeemed people (vv. 19-23). Paul prayed that we would see the transmission of the great power of God toward the believers. This great power operated in Christ in raising Him from the dead, in seating Him at the Father's right hand far above all, and in subjecting all things under His feet. This power also gave this resurrected, uplifted Christ to be the Head over all things. God's great power is now operating within us and upon us. This power was wrought in Christ, making Christ the Head over all things for the transmission of this power to the church, the Body of Christ, the fullness of the One who fills all in all.

We need to realize that God's nature, God's life, Christ's element, and the Spirit's essence have been imparted into us. Furthermore, there is a power toward us. God's power toward us is surpassingly great (v. 19). This power is a divine transmission that raised Christ up from the dead, uplifted Him to the heavens, subjected everything under His feet, and gave Him to be the Head over all things. This transmission may be likened to a current of electricity. That current is a transmission of electric power from the power plant.

In addition to the divine impartation, the divine dispensing, there is such a divine transmission. The dispensing of God the Father's nature and life, of God the Son's element, and of God the Spirit's essence is intrinsic and is within us to touch our being. The transmission of the divine power is both within us and outwardly upon us to empower us. We have the threefold dispensing within us, intrinsically strengthening us within. We also have the divine power "electrifying" us to empower us. The Body of Christ is the issue of the inward imparting of the Triune God into our being and also the issue of the inward and outward empowering of the divine transmission of God. We are those enjoying the threefold dispensing and the onefold transmission. The church is the issue of the dispensing of the Triune God and of the transmission of the empowering God.

CHAPTER TWO

THE NEW MAN
CREATED BY CHRIST IN HIMSELF
AND ENLIVENED BY GOD WITH CHRIST AS LIFE,
AS THE POEM, THE MASTERPIECE, OF GOD

Scripture Reading: Eph. 2:14-22, 4-10

OUTLINE

I. Created by Christ—Eph. 2:14-22:
   A. In Himself as the sphere and element substantially—v. 15.
   B. By slaying the enmity (the issue of the different ordinances in living and worship) through the cross—v. 16b.
   C. Putting the two (Israel and the Gentiles) into one Body—v. 16a.
   D. To be God's household and God's kingdom—v. 19.
   E. Being built together into a dwelling place of God in spirit—vv. 20-22:
      1. Upon the foundation of the apostles and prophets—v. 20a.
      2. With Christ as the joining cornerstone—v. 20b.
II. Enlivened by God—vv. 4-10:
   A. With Christ as life organically—vv. 5-6:
      1. Making the members (constituents) of the new man alive together with Christ—v. 5.
      2. Raising them up together with Christ—v. 6a.
      3. Seating them together with Christ in the heavenlies—v. 6b.
   B. By grace through faith—v. 8:

  1. By grace—by having the processed Triune God dispensed into the believers.

  2. Through faith—through Christ moving in the believers as their faith, their substantiating ability to apprehend the divine favor given to them in Christ.

C. To be the poem, the masterpiece, of God—v. 10:

  1. To show forth the wisdom in God's grace—cf. v. 7; 3:10.

  2. And to have a new man walk in the good works which God prepared for him beforehand.

D. That God might display in the ages to come the surpassing riches of His grace toward the believers in Christ—2:7.

Prayer: Lord, we thank You that You have brought us back again by gathering us into Your name. We trust in Your blessing. You helped us last night in one way. This morning we look unto You for further help maybe in another way. Thank You, Lord Jesus. You are the One in whom we trust all the time. We needed You yesterday, and this morning we need You again. We need You every moment. Be with us. Show us Your presence. May You be so dear and so near to us. Each one of us needs Your presence. Visit us, Lord. Visit us with Your mercy, grace, blessing, light, life, strength, and power. Thank You, Lord Jesus, You are the Head. You are the Lord of all. You are God's centrality and universality. You are our center and our everything. We trust in You for this meeting. Amen.

THE REVELATION OF THE BODY OF CHRIST
IN EPHESIANS 1

Before going on to see the revelation of the Body of Christ in Ephesians 2, I want to share a further word on this revelation in Ephesian's 1. I have shared messages on the book of Ephesians in conferences and trainings probably more than ten times in diverse places. We may feel that Ephesians is a familiar book to us. Some may wonder why we need to come back to Ephesians again. To explain this I would like to use the illustration of our physical body. To know the outward features and appearance of our body is easy, but to know the intrinsic composition and structure of our body is difficult. The medical field is very difficult because there are many intrinsic, mysterious things in a person's body. It is easy for us to declare that the Body of Christ is the fullness of the One who fills all in all. Even a second grader can say this, but what does it mean? I do not have the confidence that we understand this. We need to see what the Body of Christ is intrinsically. My burden is to help us all to get into an intrinsic view and an intrinsic apprehension of the Body of Christ.

The Intrinsic Constitution of the Body of Christ

I would like to summarize what we covered in the previous

chapter. We saw God the Father's impartation into His chosen and predestinated people. God the Father's impartation is of two items. First, God the Father imparted, dispensed, His nature into us. We know this because Ephesians 1:4 says that God chose us in Christ "before the foundation of the world to be holy." The phrase *to be holy* indicates that God has to put His nature into us. God, however, did not put His nature into us in a wild way. He did it in a planting way. God has planted His holy nature into our being.

In the previous message, we pointed out that only one in the whole universe is holy. Holiness is nothing less than God Himself. Holiness is God. Then how could we be holy? The only way is for God to plant Himself into us as a small seed. At the moment we believed in the Lord Jesus, God the Spirit planted or sowed Himself as a little seed into our being. This little seed is organic. Any organic seed of life grows and increases. It is the same with God as the seed within us. This divine seed grows within us gradually until our whole being is sanctified. Eventually, we will be saturated wholly with God's nature as the seed. Very few Christians have ever seen this. Some may have seen that God's choosing is to make us holy, but they have not seen that to be made holy by God implies that God has to plant, to sow, Himself into us as the very seed of holiness. This is a great thing.

God created us without the element of holiness, but He intended to make us holy. In order to make us holy, God had to take a second step after the first step of the old creation. God had to take a second step to make the new creation out of the old creation. Before I was saved, I was a part of the old creation of God. God was not in me. But one day when I was nineteen years old, I turned to God and opened up myself to Him. At that moment God sowed Himself into me. God planted Himself as a small seed into my being. The holy nature of God came into me as a small seed, and that seed is organic.

I would like to give a testimony as an example of the growth of God's holy nature within us. When I was young, I was fond of playing soccer. A few years after I got saved, I was playing soccer, and the ball came to me. When it reached me, I stopped. I could not kick the ball. Something within me turned away, so I walked off the playing field. People wondered what happened to me. They may have thought I was sick, but I was not sick. The living, holy seed of the divine nature had been growing within me, and this living, organic divine nature did not agree to kick the ball. I wanted to kick the ball, but another element within me, another person within me, would not go along with me. Instead, I had to go along with Him, so I walked off the playing field. This is the Christian life.

The Christian life is not a matter of outward regulations. We live the Christian life by something organic growing within us. By the growth of the seed of holiness within me, I was sanctified from playing soccer. From that day, when I walked off the playing field about sixty years ago, I never played soccer again. There is not a verse in the Bible that says Christians should not play soccer. But the One who was growing in me would not play soccer. I wanted to play, but He did not. This was the growing of the holy God within me. This is something precious.

Ephesians 1:4 says that God chose us to be holy, and verse 5 says that in choosing us, He predestinated us unto sonship. Why did God predestinate us? Why did God put a mark on us to indicate that we belong to Him? This is because God wanted not only to make us holy as He is but also to make us His sons. How could God make us His sons? God made us His sons not by adopting us but by begetting us. He made us His sons by sowing His seed, His divine life, into our being. His divine life was sown into our being along with His nature. This divine life, after getting into us, begets us to make us the sons of God. We were not adopted by God, but we were begotten by Him. Because of His begetting, we all have become sons of God.

Now what is within us? For holiness, the nature of God is within us. For sonship, the life of God is within us. I had been reading Ephesians for many years, but I did not see this until recently. One day I saw that Ephesians 1:4 and 5 show the dispensing of God's holy nature into us and the dispensing of God's life into our being. We are human beings, but we have the divine nature and the divine life. We all need to declare, "Hallelujah! I have the holy nature of God, so I am holy. I have the divine life, so I am divine. I am a divine son of God with His divine life and His holy nature!"

Although we are a new creation, much of our being is still in the old creation. We still have the "old cocoon" of our old nature. This old cocoon comes out many times in what we do. In our daily experience, we should not forget our status as sons of God. The son of the president would conduct himself with a certain dignity because he realizes his status. We need to realize our divine status, but often we sell our divine status too cheaply. We argue and lose our temper with people. When we do this, we are not living as sons of God. We always need to be kept by remembering that we are sons of God who have God's life, the divine life, and God's nature, the holy nature. The Body of Christ is the issue of God the Father's impartation of His holy nature and of His divine life into His chosen people. This is the initiation of the divine impartation with the Father's life and nature as the source.

Then God the Son came in to accomplish redemption. Christ redeemed us out of Adam into Him, out of the world into Him, out of sin into Him, and out of death into Him. Where are we now? We are in Christ. *In Christ* is a small phrase with a great meaning. Henry Alford, in his notes on the New Testament, said that the phrase *in Christ* means that Christ is the sphere, the realm, and the element in which and with which we have been redeemed. We have been redeemed into Christ as a sphere for us to stay in and as an element for us to be made something. In Ephesians 1:7-12 we are told that we sinners, after being redeemed into Christ, have become God's inheritance, His treasure. How could sinners be God's treasure, God's inheritance? This is because we sinners are in Christ having Christ as our precious element. Before we received Christ we were absolutely worthless. David said that he was a worm (Psa. 22:6). This is what we were before we were saved, but Christ redeemed us through His blood out of what we were and put us into Himself. Now He is not only our sphere but also our element for Him to make us precious with Himself. We all have been redeemed, and now we have Christ as the precious One within us. Christ is not only a sphere where we should stay, walk, and be a Christian but also the precious element for us to be made with Him as a precious treasure to God. Thus, we sinners all have become God's inheritance. Now we can declare that we have not only God's nature and God's life but also God's element.

Something can be made with an element. Christ has made us something so precious with Himself as the element. This element is also organic. Whatever the Triune God is to us is organic. He has sown Himself into us, and His element is growing within us. Gold as a physical element is not organic, but the gold in the New Jerusalem is organic. This gold signifies the divine nature of God. All the gold in the New Jerusalem is organic and living.

The element is more intrinsic than the substance, and within the element is something even more intrinsic— the essence. God the Spirit came in, following the Father and the Son, to seal us with Himself as the sealing ink (Eph. 1:13). This is to dispense the divine essence into our being. Thus, now we have the divine nature, the divine life, the divine element, and the divine essence. We are so divine, dear saints! I hope that we can see this. I can testify that one day the Lord showed me this. In His choosing, He imparted His nature into us. In marking us out as His sons, He imparted His life into us. Furthermore, when Christ redeemed us, He redeemed us into Himself as an element with which He made us a treasure to God, an inheritance. Furthermore, because we became His possession, His treasure, His Spirit came into us as a seal, to put a mark on us. This mark is also organic.

The sealing of the Spirit is not once for all. It is still going on, and the divine ink of this sealing never dries. It remains wet. First, this divine ink saturates us deeply; we are vertically saturated. Then the divine ink spreads within us, and we are horizontally permeated. Thus, our whole being will be soaked with the Spirit as the sealing ink, and this sealing ink is the essence. Now we have the Father's nature and life, we have the Son's element, and we have the Spirit's essence—all divine.

When we are asked the following questions, we must say, "Amen." Are we holy? "Amen." Are we sons of God? "Amen." Are we a treasure, an inheritance of God? "Amen." Are we sealed by God the Spirit? "Amen." This means that we are divine. We have God's nature, God's life, God's element, and God's essence. I have put out many teachings on Ephesians in the past, but this particular point is new. This is why I am so burdened to share again on the intrinsic view of the Body of Christ in Ephesians.

What is the Body of Christ? The Body of Christ is not only composed of but also constituted with God's nature, God's life, God's element, and God's essence. The church as the Body of Christ is not a group of poor Christians who are losing their temper, criticizing one another, and fighting one another. This is not the Body of Christ. The Body of Christ is one entity constituted with God's nature, God's life, God's element, and God's essence. I hope we can see this. This is the intrinsic constitution of the Body of Christ—a constitution with God's nature, life, element, and essence.

The Triune God Operating as the Power upon Us and within Us

In addition to this intrinsic constitution, we also need power. We Christians are not common. We are very particular because we have the divine power. People cannot overcome their temper, but we can. Paul said, "I am able to do all things in Him who empowers me" (Phil. 4:13). In the One who empowered him, strengthened him, Paul could do everything.

In the past certain ones came to me, telling me that they could not live the Christian life. A brother came to me and said, "As a husband, I am charged by Ephesians 5 to love my wife. I must confess to you, Brother Lee, I just cannot love my wife." He thought that God might have made a mistake by giving him the wrong wife. He knew that a Christian husband should love his wife and should not divorce, but he said he could not make it and had no way to go on. When he asked me what he should do, I said, "You have to be a Christian." Then he said, "But I cannot make it." I responded, "You cannot make it, but Christ can make it." I told him that if we are in ourselves, we are through. But we have to realize that we are in Christ. We are in the One who empowers us, strengthens us, to be able to do everything. I encouraged him to take Christ as the One who empowers us and to remain in Him.

Husbands can love their wives in Christ, the One who empowers them. This remedy is very effective. A number of saints were helped by this kind of fellowship. They were helped to love their wives in Christ as the empowering One. Within us intrinsically, we have a divine constitution. We also have the divine power operating upon us and within us. This power is the Triune God.

Ephesians 1 speaks of the impartation of the Father, of the Son, and of the Spirit, the divine dispensing of the Divine Trinity, but it also reveals that the three of the Triune God work together to become a kind of power. The Father is embodied in the Son, and the Son is realized as the Spirit, making the Triune God a power. This power is greater than any kind of power.

The Triune God caused this power to operate in Christ in raising Him from the dead, in seating Him at the Father's right hand in the heavenlies, in subjecting all things under His feet, and in giving Him to be the Head over all things. Christ was uplifted not from the earth to the moon but to the third heaven to sit in the heavenlies. He overcame the dark power of Satan in the air. All things were subjected under His feet, and He was given to be the Head over all things to the church, to the Body. Everything the Head is, is to the Body, that is, to be transmitted to the Body.

We not only possess the Triune God as our intrinsic constitution but also as our outward and inward power. We are powerful. We have a divine, intrinsic constitution with God's nature, God's life, God's element, and God's essence. We also have the Triune God, processed and consummated, as the power operating upon us and within us to make us powerful. With this power, we can do everything. We can suffer things which others cannot suffer. We can bear a burden which others cannot bear. We can love people whom others cannot love. This is the reality of the Body of Christ.

THE BODY OF CHRIST BEING THE NEW MAN

Having the Divine Person

I am burdened to point out the intrinsic element and essence of the Body of Christ in the book of Ephesians. In chapter one of Ephesians, the Body of Christ is the coming out, the issue, of God's impartation and transmission. In chapter two the church as the Body of Christ is the new man (v. 15). For the church as the Body of Christ there is the need of life, but for the new man there is the need of life plus the person. A body has life, but a man has life plus the person. Thus, the church is not only the Body which has the divine life but also the new man who has God as his person. To the Body, God is life; to the man, God is a person. Within us there is not only the divine nature, the divine life, the divine element, and the divine essence, but also the divine person. We have a person in us.

Created by Christ

In the whole universe, there are only two men. One is the old man, and the other is the new man. The old man is the man in Adam, and the new man is the man in Christ. We believers are not the man in Adam, but the man in Christ. Now I would like to ask how this could be. How could we become a new man? In Ephesians 2 we are told definitely that Christ created the Jewish believers and the Gentile believers, the two, into one new man (v. 15).

Before we were put into Christ, we were all old men. We need to realize that in Adam we are six thousand years old. We are as old as Adam. When Adam lived in the garden, we were there. When Adam ate the fruit of the tree of the knowledge of good and evil, we ate it also. We are not only old; we are ancient. We are "antiques." But in Christ, all these antiques were chosen by God. He has chosen all of us antiques, and He marked us out. Then Christ came to accomplish the Father's purpose, and He put all these antiques in Himself, using these antiques as materials and creating them, Jews and Gentiles, in Himself into one new man.

We need to see how Christ created us. He put all of us

antiques into Himself. First, He brought us, all the antiques, to the cross to cross us out, to crucify us, to terminate us. As the old creation, we all have been crossed out by Christ on the cross. Through His cross He has annulled, abolished, all the differences among the antiques. The ordinances, the forms or ways of living and worship, divided the Jews and Gentiles. One Jewish lady told me that if a kitchen utensil had been used for eating pork, she could smell the pork on that utensil even if it had been washed. Religious Jews, of course, do not eat pork, but the Gentiles eat pork and many of them are a constitution of pork. Then how could the Jews and the Gentiles be one? The ordinances in the Old Testament law made this, humanly speaking, an impossibility. But Christ on the cross has not only abolished the ordinances concerning pork; He has also terminated all the people who eat pork and all the people who hate pork. All Jews and Gentiles have been terminated. All ordinances have been abolished. In the church life we have people of five colors among us—white, black, yellow, brown, and red. However, we are still one. We are one because we have been terminated. Christ has terminated us on the cross. This was done within Him as the element.

Christ's death was different from anyone else's death. No human being works when he is dying, but Christ was different. While Christ was being crucified, He was working. The Jews crucified Him, but the Bible says that Christ abolished and created. Christ abolished the ordinances and created the Jewish and the Gentile believers in Himself into one new man. Christ did a work on the cross. While He was dying, He was working. When He was working there to terminate us, He put into us something of Himself, which is His element of the resurrection life. Resurrection life could never be applied to any natural man. Resurrection life could only be applied to the crucified ones. When we were crucified, Christ as the resurrection life, as the divine element, was applied to us. Now the ones who have been terminated through Christ's cross have something of Christ as the element in resurrection.

While He was on the cross terminating us, He was also putting something of Himself as the divine element in resurrection into our being. When we passed through termination on the cross, we became a new man with Christ as the element in resurrection. His cross could terminate us, but His cross in itself could not make us one. There must be something in addition to the cross. This is His resurrection life. His resurrection life is the best "glue" that sticks us all together. The cross clears up and terminates all the negative things, while His resurrection life is the best glue to stick us together. Then we all become one new man. Through the cross we became clean, and in His resurrection life we were glued together. Nothing can separate us in resurrection.

On the cross Christ crossed all of us out. He purged us, cleansed us. We are clean. Then He put this clean material into His resurrection life, and this resurrection life glued us together to make us one entity. First, this one entity is the Body; second, it is the new man. This is Christ's creation. By doing this, He "hit two birds with one stone." First, He created a new man; second, by creating us, the Jews and Gentiles, into one new man, He reconciled us all, Jews and Gentiles, in one Body (v. 16). This indicates that the one new man is the one Body.

Ephesians 4 says that all the members, all the parts, of the Body are joined together by the joints of supply and knit together by every part functioning in its measure (v. 16). We are doubly stuck together through the joints and the parts of the Body of Christ, the new man. The new man is composed of the Head and the Body. The Head is Christ; the Body is the church. The Head and the Body joined together are the new man.

Enlivened by God

Ephesians 2:14-22 reveals that the new man was created by Christ. Ephesians 2 has another part, verses 4-10, which tells us that this new man created by Christ on the cross with Himself as the resurrection element needs a kind of intrinsic constitution. When we were the old man, we were dead in our offenses and sins (v. 1), but we were enlivened by God with Christ as life organically (vv. 5-6). We are speaking of things that the people in the world and even many Christians could not understand. Yet we are talking about the spiritual, divine realities and facts.

When Christ was creating the Jews and Gentiles into one new man, no doubt, He used His resurrection life as a kind of element to join all the parts together. Meanwhile, God also did something. Ephesians 2 tells us that two were working on the cross. First, it tells us that Christ was creating. Second, it tells us that God was imparting the divine life into these dead parts to make them alive. While Christ was creating, God was enlivening.

The second part of Ephesians 2 tells us only that Christ created us into one new man by crossing out the dirt of the old man and by sticking together all the parts with His resurrection life. But how did the divine life get into the new man? The first part of Ephesians 2 shows that while Christ was creating, God was enlivening. We were dead in trespasses and sins, so God made us alive together with Christ (v. 5). He raised us up together with Christ and seated us together with Christ in the heavenlies (v. 6). He subjected all things other than Christ under our feet and gave Christ to be the Head over everything for us, making us a part of the Head. This is God's enlivening. While Christ was creating, God was enlivening for the creation of the new man. This new man has been raised up and uplifted. All things have been subjected under the feet of this new man, and the Head of this new man is over all things. The new man in resurrection as the new creation is full of newness and full of life.

If we are the church, we should have nothing old. The church is altogether a new item. The oldness has all been crossed out, purged away by Christ's death, and Christ has put Himself as the resurrection life into the crossed out ones to be their divine element. Thus, all of us old antiques have become a new man. While Christ was creating, God came in to inject, to enliven, to dispense, Christ as life into us. Christ was creating, crossing out the old man, and God was putting in the new element, that is, Christ's resurrection life. While Christ was creating, God was enlivening by dispensing the resurrection life of Christ.

On the one hand, Christ crossed the old man out and

created the new man in Himself as the sphere and element. On the other hand, God was working to inject, to dispense, the resurrected Christ as life in order to enliven the dead ones, to raise them up from the dead, to uplift them to the heavens, to subject all things under their feet, and to make them one with the Head, Christ, who is over all things. What is the church? The church is the new man. The old man has been crossed out, and Christ as the resurrection life has been added into us to make us a new man, not only having Christ as our life but also having Christ as our person. We are now one with Christ as a new man. He is our life, and He is our person.

Taking Christ as Our Person

We may understand this doctrinally, but we need to practice taking Christ as our person. When we are going to the department store, we should realize that we are not the person. We should not make a decision. We should not make a choice. We have to say, "Lord, I am not the person. You are my person. Lord, do You want to go to the department store today?" We may feel that the Lord is going with us. But we should say, "Lord, if You are going with me, I don't like this. I like to go with You. If You go, I go. It should not be that if I go, You go. It has to be—if You go, I go." The Lord may then impress us that He is not going. If He is not going, we should not go.

The sisters should follow the Lord in their shopping. A sister may feel that the Lord went and she followed. When she gets into the department store, she may find something very attractive which is on sale. At this point she should check with the Lord, "Lord Jesus, I want to buy this, but do You want to buy it? If You buy it, I will follow You." The Lord may respond, "I would never buy this." Then the sister may say, "Lord, what shall I do?" The Lord would then tell her to go back home. This is what it means to take Christ as our person. If a sister practices this, she is a new man. Otherwise, she may be labeled a new man, but she is still old. Shopping is a big test to show us what we are and where we are.

When I lived in mainland China, I wore a long Chinese

gown according to the custom of dress in China. When I came out of mainland China, I needed to change the way I dressed to the western style. I discovered what an exercise it is to dress as a member of the new man. It was not easy to buy a necktie. As I went shopping for a necktie, I took the Lord as my person, and I had to drop so many of the ties I looked at. The Lord impressed me, "If you wear this tie, you cannot speak on the platform." This shows that we have to take Christ as our person in all the details of our daily life.

Saints, are we really a new man? If we are, we have to live a life not only with Christ as our life but also with Christ as our person. Sometimes I have expressed something to my children in myself. After that I was rebuked by the Lord. The Lord impressed me that although I was a father, I was also a new man. For a new man to be a father, he must be a father in the "new man way." The children may be naughty, but a father should not respond to their naughtiness in himself. A father must be a "new man father." "A new man father" should act as a new man, taking Christ as his life and taking Christ as his person as well. The church must act as a new man. Maybe some of the leading ones in the churches argue, quarrel, and debate; that is not the new man. The leading ones should pray and fellowship together as a new man, taking Christ as their life and taking Christ also as their person. This is altogether through the cross and unto the resurrection life.

Resurrection is our home. Resurrection is Christ to be the sphere where we should stay. Then we can bear the responsibility of the church. Then we can serve God and serve the saints through the cross and in resurrection. If we live in this way, we will grow up into Christ, the Head, in all things. We can then take the lead in the church as a new man reconciled to God. Then God is living Himself out of the church. The church as the Body of Christ is the new man, taking Christ as the life and as the person.

Chapter Three

THE CONSUMMATION
OF THE BELIEVERS' ENJOYMENT
OF THE UNSEARCHABLE RICHES OF CHRIST,
AND THE EXPERIENCE
OF THE UNLIMITED CHRIST
MAKING HIS HOME IN THEIR HEARTS,
AS ALL THE FULLNESS OF
THE CONSUMMATED TRIUNE GOD

Scripture Reading: Eph. 3:2-4, 8-11, 16-19; 1:23

OUTLINE

I. The consummation of the believers' enjoyment of the unsearchable riches of Christ—Eph. 3:2-4, 8-11:
   A. God's economy of the mystery:
      1. Hidden in Himself throughout the ages—v. 9.
      2. According to His eternal purpose—v. 11.
   B. To announce, to minister, to dispense, the unsearchable riches of Christ—what Christ is and has and what He has accomplished and attained:
      1. To God's chosen people—the believers—v. 8.
      2. For the producing and constituting of the church as the Body of Christ—v. 10a.
      3. To show forth the multifarious wisdom of God—v. 10b.
   C. Through the stewardship of the apostles to carry out God's hidden economy concerning the church as the mystery of Christ—vv. 2-4.
II. The consummation of the believers' experience of the unlimited Christ making His home in their hearts—vv. 16-19:

A. God the Father's strengthening—v. 16:
1. According to the riches of His glory.
2. With power.
3. Through God the Spirit.
4. Into the believers' inner man.
B. God the Son's, Christ's, making His home in the believers' hearts through faith—v. 17a:
1. That the believers, being rooted and grounded in love—v. 17b.
2. May be full of strength to apprehend with all the saints what the dimensions—the breadth, length, height, and depth—are—v. 18.
3. And to know the knowledge-surpassing love of Christ—v. 19a.
4. That they may be filled unto, consummate in, all the fullness of God—v. 19b:
   a. As the Body of Christ, who fills all in all—1:23.
   b. For the ultimate corporate expression of the consummated Triune God.

Prayer: Lord, thank You for Your mercy that we could still be here with You. We need Your presence. Lord, You know that Your presence means everything to us. We want to meet with You, stay with You, and dwell with You in Your presence. Grant us Your rich presence. Lord, we also need You to have mercy upon us to take away all of our veils. We do not want to have anything veiling us. We want to have an unveiled face, beholding and reflecting You. Lord, give us mercy that we could see what You see and apprehend what You apprehend. Lord, reveal Yourself to us. Reveal all the secrets hidden in Your Word to us. We need this unveiling. Lord, have mercy upon us in our speaking. Oh, how much we need You in our speaking! Lord, speak in our speaking and be one spirit with us in our speaking. Lord Jesus, today is the darkest age. Vindicate Your way. Vindicate Your recovery. Vindicate Your ministry. Vindicate Your own speaking. Vindicate Your living word. Amen. Lord, defeat the enemy. We accuse him before You. We touch Your throne of authority and ask You to put Your enemy in the corner. Shame him! Glorify Yourself and bless everyone. Bless everyone who is here with You. We pray in Your mighty name. Amen.

I am very concerned for all of us. My concern is that we may read these messages and yet understand them by our natural concept. We may agree with all of the fellowship here. We may say, "What Brother Lee says is right." But it is right only according to our natural concept. We need to realize that tradition frustrates and damages us. The saints who have gone to Moscow for the spread of the Lord's recovery have seen that religious tradition still remains there. Some refused to be baptized after they believed in the Lord because they had been baptized when they were infants. Even though religion was cut off by Lenin more than seventy years ago, the Russian Orthodox tradition still remains among them.

Actually, we all have traditions which veil us from the pure divine revelation in the holy Word. You understand a certain verse in the Bible in your way, and I may understand the same verse in my way. This is because you have your tradition veiling you, and I have my tradition veiling me. Thus, I have a burden to pray, "Lord, take away all the traditions. We like to see Your Word in a pure way. We like to apprehend what You have for us according to Your realization."

THE CHURCH AS THE BODY OF CHRIST
BEING THE NEW MAN CREATED BY CHRIST
AND ENLIVENED BY GOD

Thus far, we have seen from Ephesians 1 that the church is the issue of the divine impartation and the divine transmission. In Ephesians 2 this issue is called the new man. The church is the new man created by Christ. Genesis 1 shows that the old creation with the old man was created by God directly. But the new creation was accomplished by Christ by His being crucified on the cross. While Christ was being crucified on the cross, He was not merely dying there. He was creating the Gentile believers and the Jewish believers in Himself into one new man.

In Adam we are the old creation. We are the old man. We are antique. In Adam we are all about six thousand years old. God has no intention of keeping any antiques. God does not love antiques, but God loves the newness and the freshness. As a result, God charged His anointed One, the very Christ, to bring all of the old creation to the cross. In Christ all of God's chosen people, who had become old, were brought to the cross. Satan thought that he could get rid of Christ by putting Him on the cross. But being put on the cross afforded Christ the opportunity and environment to create the new man which God wanted. He created the new man by putting the old man on the cross. Paul said that our old man has been crucified with Christ (Rom. 6:6). While He was being crucified, our old man was also being crucified. Our oldness was cleared up by Christ's crucifixion.

Furthermore, while He was clearing up the oldness, He Himself was there as the creating element. This element is never old, but ever new. He was putting this element into the new man He was creating. He crucified the old man on the cross in Himself as the element. We know according to the New Testament revelation that this new element could never be applied to us without His resurrection. His crucifixion cleared up all the oldness. Then in His resurrection His new element, the divine element, was applied to us.

While Christ was busy creating the new man, God was also busy making us dead ones alive with the resurrected Christ as life. Christ's creating and God's enlivening were in coordination. While Christ was creating the two, Jews and Gentiles, into the new man, God was enlivening. He was raising us up from the dead and uplifting us to the third heaven to be above all. Then He subjected all things under the feet of this newly created man. Furthermore, this man is one with the Head, Christ. He is Head over all things for the entire new man.

The new man includes Christ as the Head and the church as the Body. The church today is not only the Body but also the entire new man. Our physical body is not merely the part under our neck. Our physical body includes our head also. It includes everything from our hair down to our feet. The new man is Christ and the church. These two are one man. Whatever the Head is and has is for the Body. The Body can never be separated from the Head. Actually, a man's body is his entire physical being. The new man includes Christ as the Head and the church as the Body.

THE CHURCH AS THE BODY OF CHRIST
HAVING NOTHING TO DO WITH OUR NATURAL LIFE,
OUR OLD MAN, OUR FLESH, AND OUR SELF

Thus far, we have seen the intrinsic view of the Body of Christ in the first two chapters of Ephesians. Under the revelation which we have picked up from these chapters, we all should be clear that the church as the Body of Christ has nothing to do with our natural life, our old man, our flesh, and our self. The real situation in all the churches, however, does not yet match this revelation.

We need to be people who exhibit Christ according to *Hymns,* #864—"Let Us Exhibit Christ." But when the brothers come together to talk about church affairs, they may talk in a way that is full of the natural life and the natural concept. The natural life and the natural concept have nothing to do with the Body of Christ. When many of the saints come to the meetings, they like to share something; they like to prophesy. But my question to these saints is, "Do you speak outside of Christ or in Christ?" I have no intention of quenching the functioning of the saints. I am happy to hear and to see the saints sharing in the meetings. But I still have a question as to whether or not our sharing in the meetings is in ourselves or absolutely in Christ. Perhaps our sharing is seventy-five percent in ourselves and only twenty-five percent in Christ.

Sometimes in a conference the responsible brothers will ask the saints to share for no longer than one minute. This gives time for many to share. Instead of taking this fellowship, however, someone will stand up and share for three minutes. Then the elders are bothered and do not know what to do. If they stop this one publicly, that does not seem polite. To be an elder in the church is not an easy thing. They always say to one another, "What shall we do? What shall we do?" Then some of them may ask me what to do. My response also is, "What shall we do?" Many times we have no way to act because the expression of the flesh among the saints is too strong.

When a brother is sharing too long in a meeting, one of the elders may stand up to politely ask him to shorten his sharing and give time to others. Instead of listening to this elder, however, the brother will continue to share longer. Is this brother's speaking in Christ? Is his doing something created by Christ? Actually, this is altogether in the antique Adam. I have seen many things like this in the church life over the past sixty years.

In the summer of 1948, we had a conference in Shanghai for Brother Nee to resume his ministry. He had been away from his ministry for six years. One evening an older sister, who was bold, eloquent, and very outspoken, offered a prayer in the meeting. She offered a prayer which was very spiritual in wording, but her offering was fully in the flesh. This older sister was Brother Nee's mother. We did not do anything in the meeting. After the meetings, those of us who were caring for the conference would go to another room for refreshments and further fellowship. When we came together after that particular meeting, Brother Nee asked me to write a note to that older sister. I surely knew who that older sister was. I asked him to dictate the letter, and I would write what he wanted to say. He said something very strong. He told her that her prayer in the meeting was altogether in the flesh, and he asked her not to do this anymore in any meeting. He and I and an elderly sister signed this note. We all had the peace that we did the proper thing.

The next evening we were waiting to have dinner together; afterwards, we would go to the meeting hall, which was across the street. All of a sudden, we heard someone knocking on the door. The sister who was serving the dinner went to open the door. That older sister, to whom we wrote the note, was at the door. She said to the sister, "To wash people's feet is love, but the water was too hot! It burns." Then she went away. This shows that to be a good elder in the church is not easy.

It is difficult to be an elder because we members in the church often act, behave, speak, and even "prophesy" in the meetings in the old man. We are too much in ourselves. Whatever is done out from our natural life, our old man, and our self is not the Body. That is Adam. My burden in sharing these messages is to bring us some light from the Lord so that we can see what the real church life is.

What is the real church life? The real church life is the acting, the working, the behaving, the prophesying, the speaking, and the serving in the new man. The new man created by God includes the crucifixion of the old man on the cross. When the elders say that each saint should speak for no longer than one minute, we should function for no longer than one minute. When an elder stands and asks us to shorten our sharing, we should not speak anymore. We may think that this is a strong centralization of control. Actually, this is not control; this is Christ. The church is not a theater for all of us to act and to demonstrate something in the old man.

I hope that we have seen what is covered in Ephesians 2. The old man was crucified by our dear Lord. When the Lord was crucified on the cross, the old man was cleared up. From henceforth, we should have the desire not to do anything out of the old man. The Lord has crucified the old man on the cross, and His divine element has been applied to us in His resurrection. At the same time, God the Father has also worked with Him to enliven all of us, to raise us up, and to uplift us to be seated with Christ in the heavenlies. Christ's creating and God's enlivening have produced the new man.

The church life should be in the reality of this new man. The church life is a matter of Christ being dispensed into our being and being mingled with us to make us a new man, who is the mingling of the crucified, resurrected, and ascended Christ with us in our resurrected, uplifted humanity. This is the church life—nothing is of the flesh, of the old man, of the self, or of the natural life. Everything that comes out of us has to be out of Christ mingled with our resurrected, uplifted humanity. This is the way to save the church from quarreling, from arguing, from fighting, and even from division.

The church is a human entity comprising all nationalities and all kinds of people. How can we be one? If you act according to yourself, and I act according to myself, we cannot be one. It would then be impossible to practice the church life. But in the new man, the cross is here, the resurrected Christ is here, the ultimate consummated Spirit is here, and we are also here, not in the old man but in the uplifted, resurrected humanity. This is what Ephesians reveals to us as the church life. How I thank God! I am so grateful to the Lord for Ephesians. I love this book. In my old Bibles, the section where Ephesians is, is very worn because of being handled so much. We all need to see the intrinsic view of the Body of Christ in this wonderful book.

THE INTRINSIC VIEW OF THE BODY OF CHRIST
IN EPHESIANS 3

Now we need to see the intrinsic view of the Body of Christ in Ephesians 3. Chapter three is a rich, high chapter. I say this because this chapter covers two main, crucial, vital, yet sweet items. First, it reveals that the Body of Christ is the consummation of the believers' enjoyment of the unsearchable riches of Christ. Second, it shows that the Body of Christ is the consummation of the believers' experience of the unlimited Christ making His home in their hearts.

The Consummation of the Believers' Enjoyment of the Unsearchable Riches of Christ

Ephesians 3:8 says that Paul announced, ministered, dispensed, the unsearchable riches of Christ as the gospel. The unsearchable riches of Christ are now being ministered to us. We may ask, "What are the unsearchable riches of Christ?" First, these riches are what Christ is. He is God, He is man, and He is the Son. He is also the Father. Isaiah 9:6 says that Christ as the child born to us and the son given to us is the mighty God and the eternal Father. He is also the Spirit. First Corinthians 15:45b says that the last Adam, Christ, became a life-giving Spirit. Christ is also love, life, light, righteousness, holiness, power, strength, might, patience, and humility. He is the reality of all the divine attributes and human virtues. He is even our time. He was our yesterday, He is our today, and He will be our tomorrow. Christ is everything to us. He is our air, our food, our drink, our sunshine, and our clothing.

Christ also has a particular name. He is the eternal "I am" (John 8:58; Exo. 3:14). Whatever we need, He is. Do we need wisdom? The Lord would tell us, "I Am." I have told my grandchildren that they need to trust in the Lord Jesus for their schoolwork and that He is their real wisdom. Do we need patience? He is patience.

Christ's riches are not only who He is but also what He *has*. Christ has what He is. Whatever He is, He has. He is power, and He has power. Someone may think that he is a wise man, but where is his wisdom? He does not have what he claims he is. But Christ has whatever He is. He is light, and He has light. He is love, and He has love. He is life, and He has life. He is power, and He has power. What He has, is what He is, and what He is, is what He has.

Furthermore, Christ's riches are what He has accomplished, achieved, and completed. How much He has achieved! He created the universe, He accomplished redemption, He completed resurrection, and now He is in the heavens. He has also attained to and obtained certain things. He attained to the heavens and to God's eternal goal, and He obtained God's glory and honor, the headship, the lordship, the kingship, the kingdom with its throne, etc. What He is, what He has, what He has accomplished, what He has attained, and what He has obtained all are included in His unsearchable riches!

We should be those who announce the unsearchable riches of Christ as the gospel. In his first Epistle, Peter said that when we New Testament priests preach the gospel, we are telling out Christ's virtues. To preach the gospel is to announce His virtues. These virtues are the real gospel. Christ has a lot of virtues such as mercy, kindness, grace, love, and forgiveness. Do we have this virtue of forgiveness? If certain saints are offended, it seems that they will remember this offense for eternity. What husband has really forgiven his wife? What wife has really forgiven her husband? A wife may tell her husband that she forgives him, but when she speaks to her mother, she tells her mother that she could never forget what he did. The only One who can really forgive is God. To forgive is to forget. If we have not forgotten, that means we have not forgiven. Christ not only forgives our sins but also forgets our sins. This is a great virtue as a part of Christ's riches.

We need to preach Christ by telling out His virtues. Some of the trainees in our training did not know what to say when they went out to visit people. If we do not know what to say to people, that means we do not know Christ. If we know Christ adequately, we will have many things to talk about. We can say, "Dear friends, Jesus Christ is the Savior. He has many virtues. One of His main virtues is His forgiveness." Then we can go on to speak about His forgiveness. Paul said that he was assigned by God, appointed by God, to announce the unsearchable riches of Christ to the Gentiles (Eph. 3:8). The Jews despised the Gentiles, but God assigned Paul to announce the unsearchable riches of Christ to them. This assignment was his apostleship and his stewardship. This was Paul's business, his job, to carry out God's eternal economy. Paul wrote down some of what he announced in fourteen Epistles in the New Testament. The

New Testament has only twenty-seven books. Out of the twenty-seven books, fourteen were written by Paul. What an announcement these fourteen Epistles are! They are full of the unsearchable riches of Christ.

As we receive the riches of Christ, we are enriched and we become rich. When the riches of Christ are expressed, they become His fullness. The church is the fullness of Christ, the expression of Christ. Through the enjoyment of Christ's riches, we become His fullness to express Him. The church as the Body of Christ, the fullness of Christ, is the issue of the enjoyment of the unsearchable riches of Christ.

The Consummation of the Believers' Experience of the Unlimited Christ Making His Home in Their Hearts

Ephesians 3 says that the unsearchable and unlimited Christ desires to make His home in our hearts. Paul prayed for all of us that the Father of all the families would strengthen us with power through His Spirit into our inner man (vv. 14-16). We have a wonderful inner man—our regenerated spirit, which has God's life as its life. The problem is that we do not like to stay there. Instead we like to stay in our mind. A brother may remain in his mind from morning to evening, thinking about how someone has not treated him so well in the past few days. The second place we like to stay is our emotions. The sisters remain in their emotions when they go shopping, buying things according to their likes and dislikes. We also like to remain in our will. These are the three "apartments" of our "building," our being—the mind apartment, the emotion apartment, and the will apartment.

But we have a better place in which to remain. That place is our inner man—our regenerated spirit indwelt by the Holy Spirit. The human spirit and the divine Spirit are mingled together. We have such a wonderful mingled spirit within us, but we do not like to stay there. Therefore, Paul prayed that the Father God would strengthen all of us through His Spirit with power into our inner man.

In the meetings, most of us are in our inner man. But when we return home, something may offend us, and we will lose our temper in our emotion and exchange words with our spouse in our mind. While we are quarreling, we are in our emotion and in our mind. If Paul were there, he might remind us of his prayer for the Father to strengthen us into our inner man. We must turn back to our inner man. We must turn back to our spirit from our mind and from our emotion.

At times I might have wanted to exchange words with my wife, but I can testify that I did not succeed. When I began to exchange words, the One within me said, "Be quiet! Go to pray. Stop!" Suddenly I stopped and went to my room. I was stopped from exchanging words with my wife. The Lord stops us many times in this way. For a husband to argue with his wife is for him to run away from his inner man to his mind and his emotion. This is why we need the apostle's prayer for us to be strengthened into our inner man. Then Christ has the opportunity to get Himself settled, to make His home, in our hearts.

When I travel to another locality, I need to get myself settled. I need a place to put my clothes, my shoes, my pencil box, my Bibles, my reference books, my outlines, etc. I need a place to make my home. After Christ comes into our spirit, He wants to make His home in all the inner parts of our heart. Has Christ had any chance to make His home within us? Probably we have to confess that we have not given Him that much of an opportunity. But there is the possibility that Christ will have a chance to make His home in our heart. Our heart comprises the mind, the emotion, the will, and the conscience. Through regeneration Christ came into our spirit. After this, we should allow Him to spread into every part of our heart. When Christ gets the opportunity, He will spread Himself into our mind, into our emotion, into our will, and into our conscience to get Himself fully settled in our entire inward being.

When Christ makes His home in our heart, we will be rooted and grounded in love (v. 17b). By that time we will realize that our Christ is really loving. He is altogether love to us. We will be rooted in love for our growth, and grounded in love for our building up. When we are rooted and grounded in His love, we will know how to be one with all the other saints.

Then together we will have the ability and the strength to apprehend four things in the universe—the breadth, length, height, and depth (v. 18). No one can tell how broad the breadth is, how long the length is, how high the height is, or how deep the depth is. These four items are unlimited. These four universal dimensions are the dimensions of Christ. The dimensions of the universe are Christ. Christ is the breadth, Christ is the length, Christ is the height, and Christ is the depth. The very Christ whom we enjoy is marvelous, unlimited, all-extensive, and immeasurable. When we apprehend the dimensions of Christ, we will go on to know His great love, which is knowledge-surpassing. His love surpasses the knowledge in our mind, yet we can know it by experiencing it. Day by day in our experience, we can enjoy His love.

Christ makes His home in our heart, we are rooted and grounded in His love, and then we can apprehend with all the saints how broad, how long, how high, and how deep Christ is. Eventually, we can even experience a great love that is knowledge-passing. The result, the issue, the coming out of all of this is all the fullness of the processed, consummated Triune God (v. 19). The fullness of God is the Body of Christ as the expression of the Triune God to the fullest, to the uttermost. All the fullness of God is the ultimate consummation of the corporate expression of the Triune God, and this ultimate, consummated, corporate expression is the Body of Christ.

We need to realize two items in Ephesians 3. First, the unsearchable riches of Christ should be our enjoyment. Second, Christ as the unlimited and unsearchable One should be settled in us, taking our heart as His home. Then we not only have His riches, including His divine attributes and human virtues, but we also have Himself as the all-extensive, unlimited person making His home in us. This is the church life. If the church life were like this, we could not have any division among us. If the churches were like this, all the criticism would be stopped, all the opinions would be over, and all the disputes would be gone. This kind of church life annuls everything negative. This should be the goal to which we have to attain and the destination at which we have to arrive. This is why I am burdened to speak about the intrinsic view of the Body of Christ.

I have been in the church life in the Lord's recovery for about sixty years, and I have seen turmoil after turmoil among us. These turmoils take place because we are still in the old man, in the flesh, in the natural man, and in the self. When we are in the old man, there is friction among us. Divorce between husband and wife is the result of an accumulation of friction between them over a period of time. When we first come into the church life, this can be considered as the church "honeymoon" time. During this time, everything is wonderful. Later, however, the honeymoon is over. A brother may eventually feel that he does not like anyone in the church. Actually, he does not like anyone except himself. He only loves himself. This is a life in the old man, in the flesh, in the natural man, and in the self. This is a life which has never been crossed out by the crucifixion of Christ and a life which has never been brought into resurrection and uplifted to the heavens. If we live such a life, how can we have a proper church life?

The proper church life comes only from the issue of our enjoyment of the unsearchable riches of Christ. The proper church life is also the issue of Christ personally making His home in our heart to occupy every corner of our inner being. We need to have a church life which is the issue of the enjoyment of Christ's riches and the issue of the unlimited Christ personally making His home in our entire inward being. Then we can have a tranquil church life. Eventually, we will see this fully in the New Jerusalem. We will not quarrel in the New Jerusalem. This is because the New Jerusalem is the ultimate issue of our enjoyment of Christ and of Christ making His home in our hearts. The Body of Christ is the consummation of the believers' enjoyment of the unsearchable riches of Christ and the consummation of the experience of the unlimited Christ making His home in our hearts.

CHAPTER FOUR

THE MINGLING
OF THE PROCESSED TRIUNE GOD
WITH THE REGENERATED BELIEVERS AND
THE BUILDING OF THE BODY OF CHRIST

Scripture Reading: Eph. 4:4-6, 11-16

OUTLINE

I. The constituents of the divine mingling with the believers—Eph. 4:4-6:

  A. God the Father, who is over all, through all, and in all, as the origin, the source—v. 6.

  B. God the Son, who is the Lord and the embodiment of the Father, as the element—v. 5.

  C. God the Spirit, who is the realization of God the Son, as the essence—v. 4.

  D. The regenerated believers, who have believed, been baptized, and have the hope of their calling, as the human element—vv. 4-5.

  E. The Father being embodied in the Son, the Son being realized as the Spirit, and the Spirit being mingled with the believers.

  F. This mingling being the constitution of the Body of Christ.

II. The building as the consummation of the Body—vv. 11-16:

  A. The members perfected by the gifts to do the work of the New Testament ministry for the building up of the Body of Christ—vv. 11-12.

    B. That all the members of the Body may arrive at:
       1. The oneness of the faith and of the full knowledge of the Son of God.
       2. A full-grown man.
       3. The measure of the stature of the fullness of Christ (the Body of Christ—the church)—v. 13.
    C. That all the members of the Body may be no longer tossed by waves and carried about by every wind of teaching—v. 14.
    D. But holding to truth in love, may grow up into the Head, Christ, in all things—v. 15.
    E. Out from whom all the Body:
       1. Being joined together through every joint of the rich supply of Christ.
       2. And being knit together through the operation in the measure of each one part.
    F. Causing the growth of the Body unto the building up of itself in love—v. 16.

Prayer: Lord, this morning we ask You to give us a trance that transfers us from the visible circumstances into the invisible scene. We want to see something that is invisible to us. We want to see You. We want to see Your Spirit. We want to see Your economy. We want to see Your doing and Your working to dispense Yourself into our being. Thank You, Lord Jesus; thank You, God the Father; thank You, the life-giving Spirit. Thank You that You all are working within us. Especially in these days, we are enjoying Your intensified presence. Give us a trance. Amen.

RECEIVING A TRANCE TO SEE
THE INTRINSIC VIEW OF THE BODY OF CHRIST

We need to see something more than the physical universe created by God. In this universe there are two scenes, two views. One scene, one view, is visible. We can see the visible universe with the heaven, the earth, the sun, the moon, and millions of items. But the Bible shows that behind this visible scene, there is a scene which is altogether invisible to our senses. The Old Testament book of Daniel shows us these two scenes. On the one hand, the Greeks were fighting against the Persians, and the Persians were resisting the Greeks. That was seen by everybody with their physical eyes. But behind that scene were the prince of Persia and the prince of Greece. Daniel 10 records the fighting in the unseen world between Michael, the prince of Israel, and the evil princes of Persia and Greece (vv. 10-21). This is an example of the two scenes in the Old Testament.

In the New Testament Jesus came. He was altogether visible for people to see. One night a ruler of the Jews named Nicodemus came to see Him and said to Him, "Rabbi, we know that You have come from God as a teacher, for no one can do these signs that You do unless God is with him" (John 3:2). All the things which Nicodemus spoke about were in the visible realm. But the Lord Jesus answered him by telling him that he needed to be born anew to see the kingdom of God (v. 3). He told Nicodemus that he needed regeneration. At that time on earth, no one understood what regeneration was. Nicodemus did not understand because he was in the visible realm. He asked, "How can a man be born when he is old? He cannot enter a second time into his mother's womb and be born, can he?" (v. 4). The Lord spoke of regeneration in the invisible realm, but Nicodemus tried to understand it in the visible realm.

The divine revelation in the holy Word, especially in the New Testament, speaks altogether of invisible things. All the things which we have covered from Ephesians 1—3 are invisible to our eyes, invisible to our natural understanding, invisible to our natural realization, and invisible to all of our physical senses. Many readers of the Bible understand it merely according to the letter in the visible realm, but they never see anything invisible.

Ephesians is a book mainly on invisible things. In Ephesians 5 Paul charges the husbands to love their wives (v. 25), and he charges the wives to submit themselves to their husbands (vv. 22, 24). Do you think such a word is concerning something visible or invisible? Humanly speaking, everybody knows what this means. A husband's love and a wife's submission are visible to our senses. But what the apostle speaks of here is altogether invisible.

The apostle's teaching of submission is absolutely different from the teaching of Confucius. Confucius also taught submission, even a threefold submission. However, what Confucius taught is something visible, but what the apostle taught is something invisible. Why is it invisible? It is invisible because the submission taught by the apostle Paul is not a natural submission.

In herself and by herself, no wife can submit according to the apostle's teaching. The apostle's teaching of submission starts from being filled in our spirit (Eph. 5:18). To be filled in spirit with Christ causes us to overflow with Christ in speaking, singing, psalming, and giving thanks to God (vv. 19-20) and also causes us to subject ourselves to one another (v. 21). Submission comes out of being filled in spirit. This is the invisible submission.

I can testify that many missionaries who went to China understood the Bible merely in an outward, natural sense. Some of them told the Chinese that the Bible teaches the same thing as Confucius. Confucius told people to honor their parents, and the Bible says the same thing. As a young student, I said to myself that there was no need for these missionaries to come to China. We had the teachings of Confucius for years, and we did not need the same ethical teachings.

In order to be brought out of the natural concept in reading the Bible, we need a trance. Acts 10 says that one day when Peter was praying on the housetop, a trance came upon him (vv. 9-10). All of a sudden, he was in a trance. He was transferred to another sphere. In this other sphere, he saw some things, and these things were altogether invisible to the human eyes.

Do you believe the human mind can understand that our God, the Father, chose us before the foundation of the world? Long before we were born, God chose us for holiness and put a mark upon us for sonship. Do you believe that the natural mind, no matter how intelligent, understands what it is to be sanctified unto God and what it is to be made sons of God who enjoy the divine sonship? Many readers of Ephesians 1 have their natural concept about what it means to be holy as God is. Confucius also taught people to be holy, and he is considered as a holy teacher to the Chinese. But this holiness and the Bible's holiness are two different things.

The Lord Jesus told Nicodemus that he needed to be born again, but Nicodemus understood this in a physical sense. He wondered how he could go back into his mother's womb and be born again. The Lord Jesus, of course, meant something else. He was not speaking of being born of our parents with our natural life but of being born of the Spirit with the divine life. These are two absolutely different things.

When I was young, I studied the Bible and understood it nearly ninety percent according to the natural concept. It took me many years to gradually have all of my natural concepts washed away. I pointed out previously that I have expounded Ephesians many times. Thirty-eight years ago, in 1953, I expounded Ephesians in a detailed study during a training I conducted in Taipei, Taiwan for four months. However, I consider these messages today to be the top study of Ephesians. I believe that this time my natural man has been thoroughly purged of all the old concepts. All of my former understanding has been purged away with the best "detergent."

This present study of Ephesians is altogether new. Our sharing on Ephesians in the past was not wrong, but it still was somewhat in the visible view. Today everything we are sharing concerning the Body of Christ is invisible and intrinsic. This is why I had the burden to pray the prayer I offered to the Lord at the beginning of this message. We need to pray, "Lord, we ask You to give us a trance. For years we have been in the sphere of understanding Your holy Word in our natural concept and in the natural view. We need a trance that transfers us out of the natural concept into another sphere so that we can see the things which man in his natural understanding cannot see."

Previously, we saw from Ephesians 2 that while the Lord Jesus was being visibly and outwardly crucified on the cross, He was working invisibly. Visibly, He was being crucified. Invisibly, He was creating the one new man. This was a great work. We pointed out that Ephesians 2 is in two sections. According to the proper sequence, the second section (vv. 11-22) took place first. This is because Christ's crucifixion should come before God's enlivening. When Christ was crucified on the cross, we believers, both Jewish and Gentile, were included in Him and crucified with Him (Gal. 2:20). His crucifixion cleared up the oldness. Then we received His resurrection life as the element to germinate us. In His resurrection, His new element, the divine element, His resurrection life, was applied to us.

The first section of Ephesians 2 (vv. 1-10) reveals that God the Father came in to coordinate with God the Son. God the Son was clearing up the old man and the old creation on the cross, and He was creating the new man in Himself as the new element in resurrection. In the meantime, God the Father came in to enliven each one of us with the resurrected Christ as life, as the enlivening element. He made us alive, raised us up from the dead, and uplifted us to the heavens with Christ.

Who can see this? This is a record of the invisible things in the invisible world, in the invisible sphere, and in the invisible scene. We can be certain that the Triune God saw this, and that He revealed this to the apostle Paul. The Triune God gave Paul a "video" of what was going on while the Son was being crucified on the cross. Paul saw this on the "heavenly television." This is why he prayed for us that we might have a spirit of wisdom and revelation (Eph. 1:17). *Revelation* means a *video*. We need a video. For us to hear alone is not adequate; we need to see. We need to see the video of what took place when Jesus Christ was being crucified.

Actually, crucifixion was a means for Him to create us into one new man. We were crucified with Him on the cross. Then God the Father came in to enliven us with the resurrected Christ as life, as the enlivening element. While Christ was creating, God was enlivening. We need such a video, such a vision, of what took place in the Lord's death and resurrection. When we read Ephesians 2 in the past, we probably did not see such a vision. One day when I read Ephesians 2, I saw this. I did not see this vision in the past as clearly as I do now. Praise Him! Today I feel that the heavens are opened, and I am receiving a fresh vision, a heavenly video.

As a part of the new creation, I was created at the time of Christ's crucifixion and resurrection. As a part of His organic Body, I was also enlivened by God at that time. According to my human concept and feeling, I was saved sixty-six years ago. But according to God's viewpoint, I was made alive about two thousand years ago. When Jesus was crucified on the cross, I was also crucified. Then God the Father came in with Christ's resurrection life as the element to enliven me. I have seen this vision. I have a heavy burden because I want all of us to see such a vision. I am burdened that all of us would be granted by God's mercy to have a trance. We should not remain in the old sphere any longer. We must have a trance and be transferred into another sphere. We need to see what the Body of Christ is intrinsically.

In the previous chapter, we saw the intrinsic view of the Body of Christ in Ephesians 3. This chapter tells us that God the Father strengthens us with power through His Spirit into our inner man (v. 16). We should experience the Father's strengthening us into our inner man every day. Whenever I have a time with the Lord, I receive this strengthening from within. When we spend time with the Lord in prayer, we are strengthened into our inner man. Then Christ has the way to make His home in our heart. Christ's making His home in our heart is not a matter which is once for all. This should be a continuous matter. Before I come to the platform to speak, I need to spend some time in prayer to allow God the Father to strengthen me into the inner man so that God the Son can come in to get Himself more settled in my inward parts. This practice equips me to speak.

We have to see a vision of Christ making His home in His believers' hearts. This is something invisible. Who has seen this? The people in the world would think that we are speaking foolishness, but we are in a trance. We are in another field, another realm, which cannot be substantiated by our natural and physical senses. This morning when I was walking into this meeting, I had the speaking within to ask our God to give us a trance. This was a new subject for prayer. We need to pray, "Lord, we ask You to give us a trance that transfers us from the natural sphere into another sphere, the spiritual sphere." I desire to see all of us in such a trance. When we are in this divine trance, we are in Him. He Himself is our trance.

THE INTRINSIC VIEW OF THE BODY OF CHRIST
IN EPHESIANS 4

The Constituents of the Divine Mingling
with the Believers

We need a trance to see the intrinsic view of the Body of Christ in Ephesians 4. This chapter says that we need to be diligent to keep the oneness of the Spirit (v. 3). Then it continues by saying, "One Body and one Spirit, even as also you were called in one hope of your calling; one Lord, one faith, one baptism; one God and Father of all, who is over all and through all and in all" (vv. 4-6). Who understands this?

No one can understand this with their natural understanding. There are four persons in these verses—one Body, one Spirit, one Lord, and one God and Father. These four persons have been grouped together; the first one is human and the last three are divine. The Body is human, the Spirit is divine, the Lord is divine, and God the Father is divine.

Why are these four persons grouped together here in Ephesians 4:4-6? Have you ever seen such a vision, such a scene? We have seen many groups of people, but have we seen this small group of four persons—one human and three divine? We may have read Ephesians 4 many times without seeing this group of four persons. To see this group of persons is a great light. This is a vision, a video. Four persons are here, and they are all very active. The Body, the Spirit, the Lord, and God the Father are all actively being mingled together.

We may have seen something from Ephesians 4, but the scenery we have seen is imperfect. We have a broken video. We have not seen a complete, perfect view. The Spirit, the Lord, and the Father, are doing one work. They are working to mingle Themselves with the Body. Ephesians 4 presents the real scenery of the Body of Christ. This group comprising four persons—the Body, the Spirit, the Lord, and God the Father—forms a unit, and this unit, this entity, is the Body of Christ, the church. The Father is embodied in the Son, the Son is realized as the Spirit, and the Spirit is mingled with the believers. This mingling is the constitution of the Body of Christ. We all have to see this. If we see this, all the problems among the saints and among the churches will be gone. All the problems can only be resolved by such a vision.

Today among some in the Lord's recovery, there is still competition and ambition for position and for a name. This is a shameful thing to say, but it is a fact. Why are these things still going on? This is because we do not have the heavenly vision. We are short of the spiritual, heavenly, divine video. If we see this video, this video will solve all the problems. The mingling of the Body with the Spirit, the Lord, and God the Father in Ephesians 4:4-6 is invisible. Such a scene is not visible to the human eyes or realized by the human senses. This is why we need to be in a trance.

We have said that the Body of Christ, the church, is human, but it is not naturally human. The church is heavenly human. The natural humanity has been crucified, resurrected, uplifted, and mingled with the three of the Divine Trinity. We are mingled with the Spirit, possessing one hope, mingled with the Son, possessing faith joining us to Him and baptism separating us from Adam, and also mingled with the Father as the One who is over us, through us, and within us. The Body of Christ is such a mingling of humanity with divinity.

God the Father, who is over all, through all, and in all, is the origin, the source, of the entire view of the Body of Christ. He is the origin of the Body. God the Son, who is the Lord and the embodiment of the Father, is the element. The Son is mingling Himself with us by faith and baptism. God the Spirit, who is the realization of God the Son, is the essence. The Spirit is being mingled with us with a hope that one day we all will be thoroughly transformed, conformed to the image of the Son, and glorified in Him. This is the working Divine Trinity mingling Himself in a thorough way with His chosen people as the Body.

This mingling has started, but it is not yet finished. It is still going on. We have ministry meetings and church meetings to be gathered together into Christ so that we can be thoroughly mingled with Him. We are not merely attending meetings in an outward sense. Behind these meetings, there is something unseen. That unseen thing is the mingling. While we are attending the meetings, we are being mingled with the Triune God. On the one hand, we are mingling with one another. But the top mingling is the mingling of the Triune God Himself with all of us.

We surely can testify that we have more of God mingled with us in the meetings, but when we leave the meetings, we have to remain in this mingling. We need to be those who are being mingled with the Triune God all the time. This mingling solves all the problems. Two sisters may quarrel with each other because they are out of this mingling. But when they get back into this mingling, it causes them to forgive each other. Some husbands and wives may be having problems with each other. After being mingled with the Triune God in the meetings, however, their problems are resolved. The divine mingling solves all of our problems.

The Building as the Consummation of the Body

Ephesians 4:4-6 reveals a group of four persons—the one Body, one Spirit, one Lord, and one God and Father—mingled together as one entity to be the organic Body of Christ. This divine mingling is the reality of the church life. There is another portion of Ephesians 4 telling us that the members need to be perfected by the gifts to do the work of the New Testament ministry for the building up of the Body of Christ (vv. 11-16). When we are being mingled with the Triune God, we are so happy with the Lord. We love Him, and we want to do something for Him. We desire to be very useful and help-ful in the church life. How can we do this? We need to be perfected. The Lord as the Head perfects us, not directly but indirectly through His gifts—the apostles, prophets, evangelists, and shepherds and teachers. Thank the Lord that in the church we do have these gifted people. These are the ones who can perfect us.

According to our experience, this perfecting takes place mainly in the group meetings. Every church needs group meetings. The Body, the Spirit, the Lord, and God the Father are a group. They are grouped together to fellowship, to have a "group meeting." The church also needs group meetings. There should not be too many saints in a group meeting. It is better if from twelve to fifteen can come together in each group meeting.

The practice of having group meetings is according to Hebrews 10:24 and 25: "Let us consider one another so as to incite one another to love and good works, not aban-doning our own assembling together, as the custom with some is, but exhorting one another; and so much the more as you see the day drawing near." These verses show that we should not forsake our own meeting. The group meeting is our own meeting in which we come together to incite and to exhort one another. You stir up me, and I stir up you. You adjust me, and I adjust you. This is what it means to perfect.

In the group meetings, we should not have an assigned speaker. This is the clergy-laity system of Christianity. To meet in group meetings in our homes is an intimate and mutual way of meeting together. In the group meetings, all of us can receive the perfecting from the mutual asking and answering of questions.

One new brother might say that he has a problem because he does not know whether his baptism was genuine or not. Another brother may say, "I also had the same trouble ten years ago, but I was confirmed by Mark 16:16, which says that he who believes and is baptized shall be saved. The Lord showed me that this verse does not say, 'He who believes and is baptized with a definite feeling that he was genuinely baptized shall be saved.' The Lord only said, 'He who is baptized,' and I have been baptized." Then he can say to the new brother who is doubting, "Were you not baptized? Did Satan baptize you? Of course not. A dear saint baptized you. That was a genuine baptism. There is no need for you to be bothered." Then another brother may testify, "I also had the same kind of trouble many years ago. I doubted about my salvation, but I got through by standing on what the Word says. The Lord is faithful. He never will deny His Word." This is an example of the content of a group meeting.

In a group meeting there is mutual fellowship, mutual intercession, mutual comfort, mutual care, mutual shepherding, mutual asking of questions, mutual answering of questions, and mutual teaching. There is no assigned leader, teacher, or speaker. Everyone is a leader, teacher, speaker, and student. All the activities in the group meeting are in mutuality. If the saints have this kind of meeting once a week throughout the year, they will all be perfected.

Our old, unscriptural way of meeting was a waste. In the old way, a brother comes to the meeting place and sits down to wait for the meeting to begin. It is 7:25 p.m. The meeting should start at 7:30 p.m., so he waits for others to come. Eventually, everyone arrives and they are all waiting for someone to start the meeting. Now it is 7:40 p.m. The meeting has still not started because the elders are not there yet. Then one elder comes in, and this elder does not know what to do. The meeting depends on him, but he does not know how to start it. He does not know what hymn to sing, and he does not have anything to pray. Eventually, another elder comes in. Then the first elder becomes happy. The elder who came in then motions to the first elder to call a hymn. After the singing of this hymn, the first elder indicates to the second one that he should pray. After he offers a prayer, though, who is going to speak? Nobody knows. Eventually, no one speaks. Then one of the elders may ask the saints to give testimonies of their past experience. This is an illustration of the old way for us to hold a group meeting.

In the organic, new way of meeting, everyone comes to the meeting with rejoicing and singing. Isaiah tells us that when Israel returned to Zion, they came back with rejoicing and with singing (51:11). We should start our group meeting from our home by singing and praising. We may declare and sing, "Praise the Lord! This is my story, this is my song, praising my Savior all the day long." We should come to the meeting singing, praising, and testifying. All of us are the speakers in the group meeting. Such an organic group meeting is the way for us to be perfected.

Ephesians 4 says that the saints are perfected that they may do the work of the ministry, the New Testament ministry, and this ministry is to build up the Body of Christ (vv. 11-12). In the group meetings, everyone can speak. Paul said in 1 Corinthians 14 that when the church comes together, we can all prophesy one by one (v. 31). To prophesy is to speak for the Lord, to speak the Lord forth, to minister the Lord to others by our speaking. This perfects the saints.

All the saints are perfected to do the same work as the apostles, as the prophets, as the evangelists, and as the shepherds and teachers. It is by this perfecting that the church will be developed. Then the church will be growing up to have the measure of the stature of the fullness of Christ, the Body of Christ (Eph. 4:13). We will eventually be full-grown. We will no longer be little children who are tossed by waves and carried about by every wind of teaching (v. 14). We will hold to the truth in love that we may grow in everything into the Head, our Christ (v. 15). Out of Him the whole Body will grow through the functioning members, that is, through the joints of supply and through every part that functions in its measure to build up the Body (v. 16). Then the Body will be built up not by big preachers, but by every member of the Body. This means that all the Body will cause the growth of the Body unto the building up of itself in love.

In Ephesians 4:4-6, we see the mingling of four persons as a group. Then in the next section of Ephesians 4, there is the building up with a bigger group of all the members of the Body of Christ. Mingling is the beginning; building up is the consummation. We are enjoying the mingling, and we are on the way to being fully built up. Then we will reach the consummation of the completion of the building up of the Body of Christ. Now in the universe there is a building which is the top consummation of the divine mingling of the Triune God with the uplifted humanity in the heavens. This building is the consummation of the church life. The built up Body of Christ is the goal to which we all have to attain, and this is the destination at which we all have to arrive. We have to go on and on until we arrive at this destination.

There is not such a vision in the natural field. We can only see this in the spiritual view, the spiritual field. I believe that by this fellowship, we can see a video of what is taking place in Ephesians 4. The one Body, one Spirit, one Lord, and one God and Father are grouped together and are being mingled together. While this mingling is going on, we all are being perfected to do our work to build up the Body of Christ. Then the Body will be built up by itself through its functioning members. This is the intrinsic view of the Body of Christ in Ephesians 4.

Chapter Five

THE ONENESS OF THE BODY

Scripture Reading: Eph. 4:2-6, 12-16

OUTLINE

I. The oneness in reality—Eph. 4:3-6:
   A. The oneness of the one Spirit as the essence with:
      1. The oneness of the one Body—the one place to stay.
      2. The oneness of the one hope of the believers' calling—the one destination to pursue—vv. 3-4.
   B. The oneness of the one Lord as the element with:
      1. The oneness of the one faith—the one transfer into Christ.
      2. The oneness of the one baptism—the one transfer out of Adam—v. 5.
   C. The oneness of the one Father as the source, who is:
      1. Over all.
      2. Through all.
      3. In all—v. 6.

II. The oneness in practicality—vv. 13-15:
   A. The oneness of the faith—the object of the believers' believing.
   B. The oneness of the full knowledge of the Son of God—the full apprehension of the unlimited Christ—v. 13a.

III. The process from the oneness in reality to arrive at the oneness in practicality—vv. 12-16:
   A. To be perfected by the gifts unto the work of the

New Testament ministry for the building up of the Body of Christ—v. 12.

B. To grow from babyhood to a full-grown man:
   1. No longer tossed by the waves—the turmoils.
   2. No longer carried about by every wind of teaching—doctrine—v. 14.

C. Holding to truth in love to grow up in all things into the Head, Christ—v. 15.

D. To arrive at the oneness in practicality—a full-grown man—the measure of the stature of the fullness of Christ (the Body of Christ)—v. 13.

E. To be built in the Body of Christ by being joined together through every joint of the rich supply of Christ and by being knit together through the operation in the measure of each one part of the Body—v. 16.

IV. This being the best and the most effective way to keep the oneness of the Body—vv. 2-3.

Prayer: Lord, we are so happy that we have another time to look unto You for Your speaking. Lord, speak to us again. We need more unveiling. Lord, we are here. We want to see the invisible things, to see all the things in the heavens, all the things in Your heart, and all the things in Your understanding. Lord, show this to us. We are trusting in You. Thank You. Amen.

PAUL'S REVELATION OF THE INVISIBLE ASPECTS OF THE BODY OF CHRIST

Ephesians unveils to us all the invisible aspects concerning the church as the Body of Christ. We need an intrinsic view of the Body of Christ. Even our physical body can be viewed in two ways. There is an outward, external view, and an inward, intrinsic view. Outwardly, we can see some aspects of our body, but what we see outwardly is not our entire body. There is much more to see inwardly.

In October of 1938, I was in the old capital of China, Peking, and I stayed with someone who was working in the medical field. One evening he invited a group of medical doctors to eat with us. At a certain point, I asked these doctors if they believed in God. At first, no one answered. Eventually, one of them said that after studying the human body and analyzing it, they had to recognize that there must be a Creator. Otherwise, how could man have such a wonderful body with so many internal systems and organs? This doctor responded in such a way even though he was not yet a Christian. I told him that what he said was true. Even our physical body is an adequate testimony that there is a Creator.

Paul used the term *the Body* to define the church. The church is the Body of Christ. This term was not used by the Lord Jesus in the four Gospels. This is because in the four Gospels the disciples were too much in the outward view. They could not see much in an inward way. In John 14—16 the Lord tried to open up the inward things to them. In this portion of the Word, the Triune God is revealed. The Lord's speaking shows that the Father is embodied and expressed in the Son, the Son is realized as the Spirit, and the Spirit is the reality of the Son. But in John 16 the Lord told them, "I have yet many things to say to you, but you cannot bear them now. But when He, the Spirit of reality, comes, He will guide you into all the reality" (vv. 12-13a). When the Spirit of reality, the Spirit of truth, would come, He would receive of the mysterious, invisible Christ and disclose all the invisible, mysterious things He received of the Son to the disciples.

When I studied the Bible, I realized that the Spirit of truth came to Peter and his contemporaries, the early apostles, but the Spirit of truth disclosed only a certain amount to them. The main person to whom the Spirit disclosed the deep things of God was the apostle Paul. At one time, his name was Saul of Tarsus. He was a strong persecutor of Christ. While he was on the way to Damascus to persecute the Lord's disciples, the Lord Jesus, the invisible One, caught him. He called to him from the heavens, saying, "Saul, Saul, why are you persecuting Me?" (Acts 9:4). Saul then said, "Who are You, Lord?" (v. 5a). He called Him "Lord," even without knowing Him. By calling Him Lord in this way, he was saved (Rom. 10:13). In response to Saul's question, the Lord said, "I am Jesus, whom you persecute" (v. 5b).

It was to this one, later to be called Paul, that the Spirit of truth eventually disclosed many mysterious things. Paul said that he received an assignment, a charge, and a burden from God to complete the word of God, the divine revelation (Col. 1:25). It would be a great loss if Paul's fourteen Epistles were taken away from the Bible. Without his Epistles, we would not be able to fellowship anything concerning the Body of Christ. The Lord Jesus did not have the opportunity to reveal this in the Gospels.

Matthew 16 tells us that one day Jesus asked His disciples, "Who do you say that I am?" (v. 15). Peter responded, "You are the Christ, the Son of the living God" (v. 16). No doubt, Peter received a heavenly revelation of who Jesus is. The Lord went on to say that He would build His church upon this rock, upon this revelation concerning Christ which Peter received. This revelation of Christ and the church in Matthew 16 is wonderful, but it is not as intrinsic as the revelation of the church as the Body of Christ. The Lord did not tell

Peter that the church was His Body because He knew that Peter would not be able to apprehend it. Even though Peter became the top apostle in Jerusalem, he did not receive such a revelation. It was not until later that Paul received this revelation. In Paul's fourteen Epistles, we can see all the mysterious things, all the hidden things, of God's economy. This economy was a mystery hidden in God who created the universe (Eph. 3:9), but it was revealed to Paul.

As we read Paul's writings, we cannot help but wonder where and how he saw so many mysterious things. We would not be able to understand all the typology in Leviticus without his writing in the book of Hebrews. Furthermore, the Body of Christ is only mentioned in the writings of Paul. The more I have studied Paul's Epistles, the more I have wondered what kind of person he was and how he received his revelation. How could Paul see all these things? Who told Paul of the one Body, one Spirit, one Lord, and one God and Father with one hope, one faith, and one baptism (Eph. 4:4-6)?

Paul saw that in eternity past before the foundation of the world, God selected us in Christ that we might be made holy (Eph. 1:4). Who told this to Paul? In Ephesians 1 Paul told us that Christ accomplished redemption with the forgiveness of sins, and this redemption brought all of God's chosen people into Christ as a realm, a sphere, and an element. With this element we saved ones will be made God's inheritance, and eventually the entire universe will be headed up in Christ (vv. 7-12). Who told Paul this? We need revelation to see all the wonderful things revealed to Paul concerning the Body of Christ in the book of Ephesians.

THE DIVINE MINGLING AND THE BUILDING
IN EPHESIANS 4

In the previous chapter, we saw two sections of Ephesians 4. The first section of verses 4 through 6 shows that in this universe there is a wonderful, marvelous mingling of three divine persons with one human person. These verses speak of seven "ones"—one Body, one Spirit, one Lord, and one God and Father with one hope, one faith, and one baptism. These seven "ones" describe a universal, marvelous, wonderful mingling of the Triune God with His redeemed and uplifted people. The Spirit, the Son, and the Father are mingled with the Body through baptism and faith, with a hope of something to come.

Paul went on to speak more in Ephesians 4 concerning the building as the consummation of the Body (vv. 11-16). This building is by Christ as the Head, not directly but indirectly. Christ as the Victor won the battle. According to Ephesians 4:8, He captured all of Satan's captives, and He made Satan's captives His own captives. We became Christ's captives, and He brought us to the heavens. The Amplified New Testament says in Ephesians 4:8 that He led a train of vanquished foes. He led us all to the heavens. We Christians want to go to the heavens. Actually, though, we were there once already. When Christ went there, we were brought there. Christ led us all as captives to the heavens, and He presented all of us as a present to the Father. Then the Father returned us to Christ as gifts (Psa. 68:18). Christ received these gifts, one of whom was named Saul of Tarsus. The Head, Christ, then gave these gifts to the Body to perfect all the saints (Eph. 4:11-12). The apostles, prophets, evangelists, and shepherds and teachers are for the perfecting of the saints. They perfect the saints to do the work of the New Testament ministry, that is, to build up the Body of Christ.

Instead of perfecting the saints, however, the traditional practice of Christianity annuls all the functions of the members of the Body of Christ. This is why the Lord showed us the new way, the God-ordained way, to build up the Body of Christ. Thank the Lord that we have seen such a vision. We have come back to the pure Word, and we are here practicing the new way, in which everyone is being perfected to function.

The burden of this ministry is to perfect the saints to be living, active, positive, functioning members of the Body of Christ. We need to be perfected to prophesy, to speak something for God and to speak something of Christ forth into others. This builds up the church as the Body of Christ (1 Cor. 14:4b). My burden is to perfect the saints to do what the apostles, prophets, evangelists, and shepherds and teachers can do, to accomplish, to consummate, God's New Testament economy to build up the Body of Christ.

The Body of Christ is built up by our holding to the truth, the reality (Eph. 4:15). In the whole universe, what is truth? What is the reality? These four persons in Ephesians 4— the Body, the Spirit, the Lord, and God the Father—are the reality. Everything other than these four persons is vanity of vanities. Everything else is vain. In the whole universe only God the Father is real, only Christ is real, only the Spirit is real, and only the church as the Body comprising all of us is real. This is the reality to which we must hold. We must hold to God the Father, to the Son, to the Spirit, and also to the church as the Body. We must hold to this truth, to this reality, in love. Then we all will grow up into the Head, Christ. We are now in Him, but speaking truthfully, we are not in Him enough. We need to be more and more in Him. This is why Paul says that we have to grow up into the Head, Christ, in everything (v. 15).

We need to grow up into Christ in the way that we comb our hair. For many of us, the way that we comb our hair is not up to the standard of being in Christ as the Head. We comb our hair in ourselves, not in Christ. Some of the sisters spend a great deal of time to style their hair, and yet they say that they do not have time for morning revival. This shows that they need to grow up into Christ in combing their hair. When the brothers buy a pair of shoes or a tie, they should buy them in Christ. We should be in Christ even regarding the shoes and ties which we wear. We need to be those who are growing up into the Head, Christ, in all things.

When we grow up into the Head, something proceeds out from Him. Ephesians 4:16 says, "Out from whom all the Body, being joined together and being knit together through every joint of the rich supply and through the operation in the measure of each one part, causes the growth of the Body unto the building up of itself in love." To grow in life is to grow into the Head, Christ, but to operate in the Body of Christ is to operate out from Him. First, we grow up into the Head; then we have something that is out from the Head for the building up of the Body.

The Body is joined together through the joints of the rich supply and knit together through each one part functioning in its measure. Even a physical building needs steel frames as the joining factor. Then material needs to be knit together to fill up the holes between the frames. Through this joining and knitting, the building becomes a solid entity. The Body of Christ is joined together and knit together by two groups of believers—the joints and the parts. Through the functioning of all the members, all the Body causes the growth of the Body, and this growth is for the building up. The Body is built up by itself through all the members.

The first section of Ephesians 4 shows us that mingling is going on, and the second section shows us that building is going on. Thus, Ephesians 4 shows us mingling and building. Mingling is going on with the Body, the Spirit, the Lord, and the Father. The Spirit, who is the realization of God the Son, is the essence of the divine mingling with the believers; the Son, who is the Lord and embodiment of the Father, is the element of this mingling; and the Father, who is over all, through all, and in all, is the origin, the source, of the divine mingling. This mingling is the constitution of the Body of Christ.

The mingling is going on, but we all can testify that our being mingled with the Triune God is not thorough. Much of the time, the Triune God cannot get through in us. Our mind is too strong and our emotion is either too hot or too cold. How can the Triune God have the full way to mingle Himself with us? The three of the Godhead are fellowshipping among Themselves for the purpose of mingling with us. They are finding a way to mingle Themselves with persons who are so strong in their mind and fluctuating in their emotion.

The things in our environment are sovereignly arranged to help us to be mingled with the Triune God. After being married, some couples may think that their marriage was a mistake. During the time of courtship, the brother thought that the sister was wonderful, and the sister thought the same about the brother. After their marriage and honeymoon, however, both of them may feel that their marriage was wrong. This is according to the human viewpoint. But the

Lord knows that the husbands need their wives, and the wives need their husbands. This is God's assignment. Many times only the wife has a way to break the husband. This dear wife, the "wrong" wife, is Christ's cross to her husband.

Do we believe that it is easy for the Triune God to mingle Himself with us? If I want to mingle flour with oil, the flour does not struggle with me. It is "obedient" and "submissive." But when the Triune God comes to us to mingle Himself with us, do we agree? Most of the time we are like naughty children. When a mother wants to give a dose of medicine to her child, the child may refuse to take it and struggle with her. We are like this with the Lord. Who is submissive among us? Do we submit ourselves to our circumstances? Do we submit ourselves to our environment? Usually, we do not go along with our circumstances. We are not submissive. Instead, we are altogether rebellious. This is why the divine mingling of the divine persons with us does not go quickly. I can testify that the Triune God has been mingling Himself with me for over sixty-six years, but this mingling has not yet been consummated. The mingling revealed in Ephesians 4, the mingling of the Divine Trinity with us, does not go so smoothly.

Ephesians 4 shows us the divine mingling and the building up of the Body of Christ. On the one hand, the divine mingling is going on. On the other hand, the building is taking place. Mingling and building are inseparable. They are like two feet. If the divine mingling stops, the building stops. From God's side, we need the mingling. From our side, we need the building.

Much of the time we resist the Triune God's efforts to mingle Himself with us. This is why it is so difficult for the elders in the churches. To be an elder is very demanding because all of us children of God are naughty children. Sometimes I wondered why God begot so many naughty children. It seems that God chose all the naughty ones of mankind. In a meeting, we may behave ourselves as ladies and gentlemen, but when the meeting is dismissed, we immediately begin to misbehave.

Since this is the case, how can the churches be built up?

When can we see the building consummated? The mingling cannot go smoothly, and the building is very difficult. Is everything so sweet and pleasant in the local churches? Are the mingling and building going on smoothly? Is every day a clear day or a cloudy day? I would say that it is probably more than cloudy. In the church life in the Lord's recovery, we have periodic storms. This shows that we need to give ourselves to the Lord so that the divine mingling can proceed and so that the building of the Body can be consummated.

Paul received a vision of this mingling and building. He received a trance, and in that trance he saw all these things. Therefore, he prayed for us that we might also have a trance, that is, that we might have a spirit of wisdom and revelation (Eph. 1:17).

THE ONENESS OF THE BODY IN EPHESIANS 4

Now we come to the oneness of the Body. The oneness of the Body is also taught in Ephesians 4. In chapter four Paul mentioned the word *oneness* twice. In verse 3 he told us to diligently keep the oneness of the Spirit. Then in verse 13 he said that we all need to arrive at the oneness of the faith. We have the oneness of the Spirit, but we have not yet arrived at the oneness of the faith.

The oneness of the Body is the Triune God Himself. We have seen from Ephesians 4:4-6 that the Body, the Spirit, the Lord, and God the Father are one. The oneness of the Body is constituted with the Spirit, the Lord, and the Father. The three of the Godhead are one, and these three are now working in the Body to mingle Themselves with the Body. One Spirit, one Lord, and one Father are working in the Body.

In the Lord's prayer in John 17, He revealed that the Father, the Son, and the Spirit, the three of the Divine Trinity, are one. The oneness of the Body is the one Triune God. The Spirit is the reality of the Triune God, so the oneness of the Body is called the oneness of the Spirit. When we are all in the Spirit, we are one.

We need to be those who are diligent to keep the oneness of the Spirit. In a meeting a husband and a wife may sing together in oneness, but when they return home from the meeting, they may fight with each other. In some churches, the elders may fight with one another. From 1936 to 1938, I helped the church in Peking, the old capital of China. The elders in that church could not be one with one another. They called me to come and help them. When I stayed with them, they were so happy, but when I left, their problems with one another returned. I am not speaking something lightly. This is why it is hard to see a church which has been really built up among us. The mingling and the building have been held back because we are not diligent to keep the oneness of the Spirit so that we can arrive at the oneness of the faith.

Paul put the mingling and the building together in Ephesians 4. On the one hand, he presented the mingling of the Divine Trinity with His redeemed people. On the other hand, he showed us the building of the Body through the functioning of all the members. In the section of Ephesians 4 on the building, Paul speaks of his desire that we would be no longer children, no longer babes (v. 14). As we are being perfected, we are on our way to arriving at the oneness of the faith and of the full knowledge of the Son of God, at a full-grown man, at the measure of the stature of the fullness of Christ (v. 13). When we arrive at this destination, we will be full-grown. Today in the recovery, many still remain in babyhood. According to Ephesians 4:14, the babes are tossed by waves and carried about by every wind of teaching. We need to grow in the divine life until we arrive at the oneness of the faith and of the full knowledge of the Son of God.

In 1984 I realized that the churches in the Lord's recovery were in a dormant situation. Thus, I began to minister to bring the churches into the new way, the God-ordained way, to build up the Body of Christ. Because of the practice of the new way, however, some among us began to fight. Some said they were for the new way, whereas others said they were for the old way. Of course, the new way is the scriptural way, but the new way is not our faith. Neither the new way nor the old way is our faith. Whether or not we practice the new way does not determine our eternal salvation.

If we take the proper, scriptural way, however, we can gain the increase, and we can receive a reward when the Lord comes back. This reward is in addition to our salvation. If we take the old way and do not bear fruit, the Lord will ask us to give Him an account when He returns. In the parable for faithfulness in Matthew 25, the slave did not make any profit for his master and told his master that he was a hard man. The master responded by telling this slave that he was evil and slothful (vv. 14-30). This parable speaks of the reward and punishment in the coming kingdom. The profitable slaves will enter into the enjoyment of their Lord in the coming kingdom, but the useless slaves will be cast into the outer darkness.

Whether or not we take the scriptural way in this age may determine whether or not we are rewarded in the next age. But our taking the new way or the old way does not determine our salvation. Our salvation is secured, guaranteed, and eternal. Our eternal salvation is based upon the person of Christ as the Savior and upon His work of redemption with His redeeming blood. The divine person of Christ and the redemptive work of Christ are the items of our faith. If we contend for anything other than the items of our faith (Jude 3), we will be divided, and we will even become divisive.

In order to arrive at the oneness of the faith, we have to grow. All the different doctrines and practices are like toys. The new way may be one brother's toy, and the old way may be another brother's toy. One brother has his toy, and another brother has his toy. They are babyish; they are still children. They hold on to their preferences, their likes and dislikes. The more we grow, however, the more toys we drop. When I was a young Christian, I contended for some doctrines and practices as toys. But when I grew, I dropped these toys. Today I can boast that I do not have any toys.

There are many ways to drive from Los Angeles to Washington D.C. We should not quarrel about which way to take. As long as we agree with the destination, that is all that matters. The way that we take to Washington D.C. can be likened to our toy, and the destination of Washington D.C. can be likened to our faith. We should not contend for anything other than the faith.

The Southern Baptists say that you must be immersed by them in the water in their baptistry to become a member of their denomination. The doctrine of baptism has become their toy. Today we should not care where someone is baptized, and we should never contend with people about the method of baptism. If we have seen the vision of the oneness of the faith, we will drop all the toys. We should not fight about the old way or the new way because these ways are not our faith. We must keep the oneness. The troubles come because of the immature saints being carried about by the winds of different teachings, doctrines, concepts, and opinions.

The God-ordained way, the new way, is not a toy to us in our ministry. This way is the scriptural way, the organic way, to build up the Body of Christ. I have received a burden from the Lord to tell His people that the old way annuls the functions of the members of the Body of Christ. In the old way, the Head is cut off and the parts of the Body are annulled. All that is left is a relatively small number of clergy. This is why we have to put the old way aside. We want Christ, but we do not want the religious system of Christianity. The "-anity" should be cut off, and we should only take Christ. We must come back to Christ and to His Body with all the members functioning. This is not my preference. This is the God-ordained way to build up the Body of Christ.

We all have to see that the Triune God is mingling Himself with the Body. This mingling is still going on. Furthermore, the faithful gifts—the apostles, prophets, evangelists, and shepherds and teachers—are doing their best to perfect the saints. They are doing their best to teach the saints, to instruct them, to equip them, and to give them some direction, some way, so that they can do the work of the New Testament ministry to build up the Body of Christ. Then the whole church will be geared to function. The joints will be supplying to join the Body together and the parts will be operating to knit the Body together. Then the Body will be built solidly.

The building matches the mingling. Actually, the mingling and building are one. Without the mingling, we cannot build. Without the building, the mingling can never be consummated.

The mingling and the building will result in the completed, consummated church as the Body of Christ.

I hope that we all can see this. Paul saw a vision. He had a proper, actual trance, to get out of the old concept and into the new concept. He saw all these things, and we have to thank God that what Paul saw was put down in writing. We thank the Lord for this book of Ephesians! If we did not have this book, we would have no guide, no direction, and no light concerning the details of the Body of Christ. We would not be able to see the intrinsic view of the Body of Christ. But thank the Lord that we have the guide, the direction, and the light. We can see the mingling of the processed Triune God with the regenerated believers and the building up of the Body of Christ. We can also see the oneness of the Body of Christ with the oneness of the Spirit and the oneness of the faith and of the full knowledge of the Son of God. May the Lord have mercy upon all of us that our eyes would be fully opened to see the intrinsic view of the Body of Christ.

Chapter Six

DIVISION DAMAGING
THE ONENESS OF THE BODY

Scripture Reading: 1 Cor. 1:10-13; 3:3-4; 4:6; 11:17, 29-30, 19; 12:24-25; Eph. 4:2; Rom. 16:17; Titus 3:10; Lev. 13:45-46; Num. 12:10-15.

OUTLINE

I. Divisions being among the Corinthians—1 Cor. 1:10:
   A. All not speaking the same thing.
   B. Not being attuned in the same mind and in the same opinion.
   C. Having, rather, jealousy and strife—1 Cor. 1:11; 3:3.
   D. Making parties by saying, I am of Paul, I am of Apollos, I am of Cephas, and I am of Christ—1 Cor. 1:12.
II. Such divisions being condemned by the apostle's teaching:
   A. Being fleshly and walking according to man—1 Cor. 3:3-4.
   B. Is Christ divided? Was Paul crucified for you? Or were you baptized into the name of Paul?—1 Cor. 1:13.
   C. Being puffed up on behalf of the one, against the other—1 Cor. 4:6.
III. Such divisive ones coming together to take the Lord's table not for the better (not for profit) but for the worse (for loss)—1 Cor. 11:17:
   A. Not discerning the bread as a symbol of the Lord's physical body that needs to be regarded by them.

B. Not discerning the bread as a symbol of the Lord's mystical Body that requires them to keep the oneness of the Body of Christ.

C. Eating judgment to themselves—1 Cor. 11:29.

D. Because of this, many among them being weak and sick, and a number sleeping—1 Cor. 11:30.

IV. Parties of division manifesting those in the church life who are approved—1 Cor. 11:19.

V. Having the same care for all the members to avoid division in the Body—1 Cor. 12:25.

VI. No base, no reason, no excuse, no justification, and no vindication for any kind of division.

VII. Always remember: there is no way for the members of the Body of Christ to be legitimately divided in the Body of Christ!

VIII. All problems can and should be solved through proper and adequate fellowship by praying together sincerely and thoroughly:

A. By seeking the Lord's solution with an open spirit, a pure heart, a lowly mind, and a meek attitude— Eph. 4:2.

B. According to the teaching of the Scriptures properly interpreted, not understood by taking them out of context.

C. Without self-interest; the entire pursuit being for the Lord's glory and for the benefit of the Lord's recovery.

D. No parties or divisions formed for backing in partiality, threatening, and/or challenging others.

IX. Dealing with divisive members:

A. Turning away from division-makers—Rom. 16:17.

B. Rejecting factious, sectarian, members—Titus 3:10.

C. Practicing the quarantining of the lepers in typology—Lev. 13:45-46; Num. 12:10-15.

Prayer: Lord, how we thank You. We thank You that You have brought us to this last meeting. We praise You that You are the Alpha and the Omega. We believe that You have blessed the beginning and that today You will bless the ending. We trust in You for this last meeting. This is the last day as the great day. In a great day, Lord, come to bless us greatly. Lord Jesus, we need You every moment. We can never forget You. You are in our mind, in our spirit, in our heart, and in our whole being. Thank You, Lord Jesus. You have the Word and You are the Spirit. Both Your Word and Your Spirit will always be with us. Amen.

In this chapter we want to continue our fellowship concerning the oneness of the Body. Then we want to see how division can damage this oneness.

THE ONENESS OF THE BODY

In Ephesians 4 two aspects of the oneness of the Body are unveiled—the oneness in reality and the oneness in practicality. The oneness of the Body is not merely a doctrine but a reality. This oneness is more than a oneness among all of the believers and among the local churches. It is a oneness of the Triune God, existing among the three of the Godhead. There is one God, yet His Godhead is three. Thus, He is the three-one God, the Triune God. Among the three of the Godhead there is an eternal oneness. God the Father is one with the Son and with the Spirit, the Son is one with the Father and with the Spirit, and the Spirit is one with the Son and with the Father. All of the three are one with one another.

Furthermore, this wonderful, divine oneness among the three of the Godhead has been increased. The Lord Jesus told us that as the one grain of wheat, He fell into the ground to die so that He could bear much fruit (John 12:24). Thus, the one grain has become many grains. The many grains are an increase to the one grain.

In eternity past the Triune God did not have children. This means that He did not have an increase. One day, He created man, and the man He created was multiplying and increasing all the time to replenish the whole earth (Gen. 1:28). However, the Triune God Himself was still childless. Four thousand years after His creation of man, He was incarnated, putting on the human nature to be a man. Even at that time, however, He was still childless.

When did the Triune God beget His many children? This took place in the resurrection of Christ. This resurrection was a great birth, a great delivery. In that great delivery in resurrection, Jesus, who was already the only begotten Son of God from eternity (John 1:18; 3:16), was begotten to be the firstborn Son of God among many brothers (Acts 13:33; Rom. 8:29). Now the Triune God has millions and millions of children. In resurrection Jesus is the firstborn Son of God, and we are His many brothers. The firstborn Son and His many brothers were all delivered on the same day, at the same time. First Peter 1:3 says that when Christ was resurrected, we all were regenerated. In His resurrection, He imparted the divine life into us to make us His brothers and the many sons of the Triune God.

This great delivery, this great birth, of God's firstborn Son and His many brothers took place on the day of resurrection. But in another sense, in the process of time, this delivery has not been fully consummated. It is still going on in time. Whenever the local churches gain some increase, that is the continuation of that unique delivery. It will go on and on until the record in the heavens is fulfilled. This great, universal delivery will be fully consummated, completed, when the Lord comes back. The many sons of the Triune God are His increase. Thus, the oneness of the Triune God has also been increased to include His sons, the members of His Body.

At one time this oneness was only among the three divine persons of the Godhead, but now it has gotten into millions of believers. These millions of believers, the many sons of God, are the corporate Body of Christ. Millions and millions of believers are incorporated in this corporate Body. Now we can see how great this oneness is.

In the local churches, we have believers from every continent and of all races, of all colors. Instead of quarreling, we are singing together and praising together. How wonderful this oneness is among us! But the oneness we enjoy is just a miniature of the great universal oneness of the entire universal Body of Christ. This oneness was merely among the three of the Godhead in eternity past. Now it has been expanded, enlarged, and increased to include the millions and millions of sons of God who are the members of the great universal Body of Christ. We are now testifying of this oneness.

We believers are one with the Triune God. Man can be one with God because he was created after God's "kind." Genesis 1 tells us that in God's creation, everything was created after its kind. Man is after God's kind because he was created in God's image and after God's likeness (v. 26). We are not God, but we bear God's image and even have God's likeness. We are the photos of God. We say that we are mankind, but we need to realize that mankind is after God's kind.

Those created men who were chosen by God were born of Him to become His children. We have been born of God, and God is now our Father. The children of a father are the same as their father in life, but they are not the same as he is in his fatherhood. Only he is the father. They are the children. In the same way, as the children of God, we are the same as God because we have His life and nature. However, we are not the same as God in His Godhead or in His fatherhood. As the children of God, we are one with our Father God.

The Oneness in Reality

The Oneness of the One Spirit as the Essence

Ephesians 4:3-6 reveals the oneness in reality. The oneness in reality is the oneness of the one Spirit as the essence with the oneness of the one Body—the one place to stay. We all stay in this one Body. Moreover, God the Father stays here, God the Son stays here, and God the Spirit stays here. Spiritually speaking, we all are staying in the oneness of the one Body with the Triune God. Thus, the Triune God is staying with us. The Spirit is the essence of the oneness, this Spirit is staying in the one Body, and the one Body is our lodging place.

This oneness is also the oneness of the one hope of the believers' calling—the one destination to pursue (vv. 3-4). Where are we going? What is our destination? The coming

Christ is our destination. Our destination is a wonderful person. He is here, yet He is coming. He is here as our hope, and He is coming as the goal of our hope. We are all on the same way to arrive at the same destination. We may have the intention of coming back to Reston, Virginia for another conference next year. We may feel that this will be our destination. But suppose the Lord Jesus returns two months before that time. Will we say, "Lord Jesus, wait a while; we haven't arrived at our destination yet"? I am illustrating in this way to show us that our destination every day, every morning, and every moment is the coming Jesus. Today He is our hope, and we are pursuing Him as our one destination. He is our goal, He is our hope, and eventually we will arrive at Him as our destination. Millions and millions of Christians all have one destination. We will all be together to meet our returning Lord.

The Oneness of the One Lord as the Element

The Spirit is the essence of the oneness, and the Lord is the element of the oneness. The essence is in the element. The oneness in reality is the oneness of the one Lord as the element with the oneness of the one faith—the one transfer into Christ. Faith transfers us into Christ. We used to be in Adam, but faith transferred us into Christ.

The oneness of the one Lord as the element is also with the oneness of the one baptism—the one transfer out of Adam (Eph. 4:5). Baptism is a transfer on the negative side. It transfers us out of Adam. It is terrible to be in Adam, but how can we get out of Adam? Faith joins us to Christ and baptism separates us from Adam. This is why we have to believe and be baptized (Mark 16:16). We have to get out of Adam and get into Christ. Baptism gets us out of Adam, and faith gets us into Christ. The one Lord with one faith and one baptism is a base of our oneness.

The Oneness of the One Father as the Source

The oneness in reality is also the oneness of the one Father as the source, who is over all, through all, and in all (Eph. 4:6). Paul described the oneness in such a fine way. He showed us that God the Father is the source of our oneness, the Lord is the element of our oneness, and the Spirit is the essence of our oneness. The Father as the source, the origin, is now over us, through us, and in us. He is the saturating One and the permeating One. Actually, the Father Himself is triune. He is the triune Father because He is in three directions—over all, through all, and in all. *Over all* refers mainly to the Father, *through all* to the Son, and *in all* to the Spirit. The Father, the Son, and the Spirit are the source, the element, and the essence of the oneness in reality.

We need to be in a trance to see this. We do not want to remain in the natural field. We want to be in a trance, in an invisible sphere, to see the invisible reality of the oneness of the Body of Christ. When we are in such a trance, we can see Christ in one another. Why are we one? Why do we sing the same and pray the same? Although we are of different races and from different places we are one because the same One is over us all, through us all, and in us all. We are in something that is invisible—the oneness in reality.

When we were born again, we were immediately delivered into this oneness. When a child is born, he is delivered into a family and becomes a member of that family. In the same way, when we were born again, we became members of God's family. Recently, a Russian couple came to a church meeting in Anaheim and asked how they could become members of our church. I dared not to disturb the meeting, but within me I said, "You have already received your membership." After being delivered, a newborn son has already received his sonship, his membership into his family. Since we have been born of God, we all are members of the great oneness of God's family. This is the reality, and we are in this reality.

After we have been regenerated, however, we Christians have a long way to walk, a long way to go. I have been on this way for over sixty-six years. The longer the way is, the more trouble there is. Today we may all be happy. We may declare, "Hallelujah! We are one!" Later, however, a "barking dog" may trouble us. In Philippians 3:2 Paul told the Philippians to "beware of the dogs." These dogs were the religious Judaizers.

Today you may be so happy in the enjoyment of the divine oneness, but later someone may come to poison you with doubts, rumors, and other negative things. They may even give you some negative literature to read. Then you will wonder, "Is the local church like this?" You may then begin to think that you came to the wrong place and that you were born into the wrong family. By receiving these negative things, your enjoyment of the oneness has been cut off. This one who came to you from outside the recovery may be considered as an "outdoor barking dog."

There are also those from within who may be considered as "indoor barking dogs." One of them may ask you where you meet. Then he may ask you if you know a certain brother there. When you say that you do, he will begin to tell you many things about this brother. Then when you go to your next meeting and see this brother, the sight of his face will quench you. Your feeling and attitude toward him will have been affected, and your oneness with him will have been damaged.

There is much barking today to distract us from the oneness of the Body of Christ. Much of this barking comes from the religious world. We pointed out previously that the saints who have gone to Russia for the Lord's move have seen that the Russian Orthodox tradition still remains there. Some refused to be baptized after they received the Lord because they had been baptized when they were infants. Although religion was cut off in Russia by Lenin more than seventy years ago, the "barking" of traditional religion still remains. This barking can distract the proper, normal Christians from the way of the oneness of the Body. On our Christian way, there is much barking to distract us.

Sometimes the wives can speak things to distract their husbands. A wife may say, "In the past we used to attend every meeting. But now I don't like to go to the church meetings too often." The husband then may ask, "Dear, what is the reason?" She may then say that two of the elders are not very nice and that she does not like to see them. Such speaking will spontaneously, secretly, and hiddenly distract her husband. By receiving this speaking, her husband will be cooled down in his feeling toward the church.

How can we overcome all of this barking? The invisible vision keeps us. Paul told King Agrippa, "I was not disobedient to the heavenly vision" (Acts 26:19). Paul did not disobey the heavenly vision which he had received. Vision keeps us. Vision strengthens us. The barking cannot affect us because we have seen something so real. I hope that all of us will see a vision of the real oneness in this universe. If we see such a vision, we will not be distracted by anything. We will not be distracted by the division and confusion in Christianity. We will only care for what we have seen in the trance. Through these messages, the Lord has brought us into a trance. In this trance, we have seen the oneness in reality. We see that we have to remain in this oneness because we were born into it.

The Oneness in Practicality

The other aspect of the oneness is the oneness in practicality. All of the believers in Christ were born into the oneness of reality, but we all need to go on until we arrive at the oneness in practicality.

The Oneness of the Faith

The oneness in practicality is first the oneness of the faith. The faith is the object of the believers' believing. To insist on anything besides the faith as a basis for receiving the believers is to be divisive. Today's denominations have been founded on something other than the unique faith, which consists of the truth concerning the divine person of Christ and His redemptive work accomplished for our salvation. The Presbyterian denomination is founded on the practice of the presbytery, the eldership. The Southern Baptist denomination is founded upon the practice of baptism by immersion. A person has to be baptized by the Southern Baptists in order to be received into their fellowship. Because they receive the saints on a condition other than that of the faith, they have become a division.

Our faith is focused on a wonderful person—Jesus Christ. He is God becoming a man to be our Savior. He died physically on the cross and shed His physical blood for our sins. He was buried for three days and He resurrected physically, psychologically, and spiritually to be the Spirit indwelling us. We believe in Him as such a person, and we believe in His redemptive work in dying for us and being resurrected.

The modernists do not believe this. They say that Christ died on the cross as a martyr and that His death has nothing to do with our sins. They also do not believe that Christ resurrected. They are not genuine believers, because they do not believe in the person of Christ or in the work of Christ as the One who died for us to accomplish redemption. We, however, are genuine believers, genuine Christians, and this is our faith.

We should not contend for anything other than this unique faith. This faith is common to all believers (Titus 1:4). We should not be distracted from this unique faith to anything else. The doctrine of the presbytery with the Presbyterians, the practice of baptism with the Southern Baptists, the methods of the Methodists, and the teachings and practices of Catholicism are examples of distractions from the unique faith issuing in divisions. Once we are distracted, we lose the peace of the oneness in reality. However, if we are diligent to keep the oneness of the Spirit, avoiding every distraction, we will be on our way to arriving at the oneness of the faith, the oneness in practicality. The more we grow in life, the more we will cleave to the faith, and the more we will drop the minor and meaner doctrinal concepts that cause division.

We need to reject every voice that distracts us from the oneness of the Body. Sometimes these voices are big, and other times they are small. A sister may tell someone, "I trusted in the church for twenty-five years, but I recently found out that some of the elders are not trustworthy. They lie." This short speaking is enough to distract and to poison others. The distracting voices can cause us to depart from the oneness in reality. Then we surely do not have the oneness in practicality. We need to reject any kind of distracting voice. We should not want to hear any distracting thing. Then we will have the peace and the joy. We will enjoy the oneness in reality so that we can arrive at the oneness in practicality.

There are many divisions surrounding us. Many gospel contacts wonder why there are so many different kinds of so-called churches since we all believe in one Jesus. In the midst of so much division and confusion, we must learn how to see the invisible things from the Word. The Word will show us the right way; the Word will assure us of the right thing; and the Word will keep us in the oneness in reality. Then we will have the proper practice of the oneness. I believe that what is practiced in the Lord's recovery is the proper oneness. We are both in the oneness in reality and in the oneness in practicality.

The Oneness of the Full Knowledge
of the Son of God

The oneness in practicality is not only the oneness of the faith but also the oneness of the full knowledge of the Son of God—the full apprehension of the unlimited Christ (Eph. 4:13). There are arguments today not only about Christ's death but also about Christ's person. The Scriptures say that Jesus Christ, as the last Adam, died on the cross for our sins and was resurrected. First Corinthians 15:45b says that in His resurrection, Jesus as the last Adam became a life-giving Spirit. This is clearly revealed in the Bible, but some rose up against us to claim that it is heresy to say that Christ is the Spirit.

A number of Christians today believe that the three of the Triune God are three gods. They believe the wrong teaching of tritheism. Tritheism, the teaching that there are three gods, is heresy. The three of the Godhead are distinct, but they are not separate. The three of the Godhead mutually indwell and live in one another. This is called coinherence. In John 14 Philip said, "Lord, show us the Father and it is sufficient for us" (v. 8). The Lord responded, "Have I been so long a time with you, and you have not known Me, Philip? He who has seen Me has seen the Father....Believe Me that I am in the Father and the Father is in Me" (vv. 9-11). This portion of the Word shows that the Son and the

Father are inseparably one. The Son is in the Father, and the Father is in the Son. Also, the Son is the Father (Isa. 9:6).

Christ is all-inclusive. He is the Son, He is the Spirit, and He is the Father. He is also a man. Because some are short in the full knowledge of Christ, there are arguments. This is why Paul says that we need the oneness of the unique faith, and we need the oneness of the full, complete knowledge of Christ. We should not be narrow-minded or short-sighted about Christ, because He is all-inclusive.

People have also condemned us because we have said that our experience of Christ may differ. But this is according to the typology in the Old Testament. One person might bring a bullock to offer, whereas another person who was poor could only bring a small bird (Lev. 1:3, 14). Both of these offerings are types of Christ, but one portion is bigger than the other. This means that one person's experience of Christ can be bigger than another person's experience. The full knowledge of the Son of God is the apprehension of the revelation concerning the Son of God for our experience. We all need to experience the all-inclusive Christ.

The four Gospels show that the one Christ has four aspects. John shows that Christ is God. In the beginning was the Word, the Word was God, and this Word became flesh (1:1, 14). Luke shows that Christ is a man, Matthew reveals that He is a king, and Mark shows that He is a slave. Christ is all-inclusive, so we have to know Him in full. We should not be narrow-minded or short-sighted about Christ.

When we are one in knowing Christ, we will have the practical oneness. If we are perfected and completed in knowing Christ, we will not suffer the loss of the oneness of reality in our practice. If we do not practice the oneness properly, we will leave the oneness in reality. Many Christians today in the denominations have left the oneness in reality. By the Lord's mercy, our eyes have been opened to see the divine oneness of the Body of Christ. We know this oneness, and we are also practicing this oneness, the oneness in reality and the oneness in practicality.

The Process from the Oneness in Reality to Arrive at the Oneness in Practicality

We were born into the oneness in reality. Then we need to arrive at the oneness in practicality. There is a process from the oneness in reality to arrive at the oneness in practicality (Eph. 4:12-16). To fully arrive at the oneness in practicality, we need to be perfected by the gifts unto the work of the New Testament ministry for the building up of the Body of Christ (v. 12). Then we will grow from babyhood to a full-grown man, no longer being tossed by the waves, the turmoils, and no longer being carried about by every wind of teaching, doctrine (v. 14). To arrive at the oneness in practicality, we need to hold to truth in love to grow up in all things into the Head, Christ (v. 15). Eventually, we will be a full-grown man with the measure of the stature of the fullness of Christ, the Body of Christ (v. 13). We will be built in the Body of Christ by being joined together through every joint of the rich supply of Christ and by being knit together through the operation in the measure of each one part of the Body (v. 16). This is the best and most effective way to keep the oneness of the Body (vv. 2-3).

DIVISION DAMAGING THE ONENESS

The apostle Paul spoke of the Body of Christ and warned the believers about division damaging the oneness of the Body. In Romans, Paul mentioned the Body in chapter twelve, saying that "we who are many are one body in Christ" (v. 5). The following book is 1 Corinthians. First Corinthians is a rich book on the enjoyment of Christ. In 1 Corinthians Christ is revealed as twenty items for our enjoyment (see note 9^2 in 1 Corinthians 1) Eventually, 1 Corinthians reveals that such a One became the life-giving Spirit. This is the twentieth item. All the foregoing nineteen items are included in this last item. If He were not the life-giving Spirit, He could never be our wisdom: our righteousness, our sanctification, and our redemption (v. 30). If He were not the life-giving Spirit, He could not have come into us, and He would have nothing to do with us in our experience. But thank Him that He is the life-giving Spirit. Furthermore, 1 Corinthians 6:17 says, "He who is joined to the Lord is one spirit." We are one spirit with Him because He is the Spirit mingled with our spirit. We have an organic union with Him in our spirit.

First Corinthians is such a marvelous book on the enjoyment of Christ, but this book also covers the negative side. It teaches us how to face division, how to deal with division, and how to avoid division. Ephesians teaches us mainly about the oneness on the positive side, whereas 1 Corinthians teaches us mainly about the oneness on the negative side.

Divisions Being among the Corinthians

First Corinthians 1:10 says that there were divisions among the Corinthians. They did not all speak the same thing. If we all speak different things, we will be divided. Furthermore, the Corinthians were not attuned in the same mind and in the same opinion. To be attuned may be likened to the tuning of a piano. The piano will not give a harmonious sound if it is not tuned. We may be likened to a piano with the mind as one key, the emotion as another key, the will as another key, and the conscience as still another key. We may not be attuned in the same mind and in the same opinion, so when Jesus comes to "play on us," we do not sound so well. Our sound is not harmonious, so we need the heavenly One to attune us.

When a brother exchanges words with his wife, or when a wife argues with her husband, that is not harmonious. This is why we need to be attuned. The Lord needs to come to touch us. He wants to touch our mind and our emotion. Our emotion should be attuned, because we are wild in our emotion. We are also stubborn in our will. Once we have decided something, no one can change us. This is why the Lord needs to attune our will, to make our will soft and flexible. I believe that many of us have experienced these things. I have been attuned often. All of us need to be attuned in the same mind and in the same opinion. Then we will become like a grand piano which plays fine music in harmony.

In Corinth it was not like this because there were jealousy and strife among the saints there (1 Cor. 1:11; 3:3). Some young sisters in the church life may become jealous of one another. When they pray, when they share, or when they prophesy in the meetings, they are competing for "amens." When one sister shares, she receives many "amens," but when another one shares, she does not receive many "amens." Then the sister who did not get many "amens" becomes offended. This is jealousy. Some will not function unless they have the assurance that they will hear many "amens" from the saints. If they do not have this assurance, they will keep silent. This shows that it is easy to have jealousy and strife in the church.

The Corinthians also made parties by saying, "I am of Paul, and I of Apollos, and I of Cephas, and I of Christ" (1 Cor. 1:12). Parties are divisions. In our local church, there may be four or five speakers who minister the word. When we come to a ministry meeting, we may ask who is going to speak. If one brother is speaking, we will not go, but if another brother is speaking, we will go. To our feeling this brother is wonderful. We are "of him." This is a party. We may think that we are merely choosing to go hear a brother who is a good speaker, and not choosing to go to hear another brother who is a bad speaker. But to do this is to make parties. We all have to learn to avoid anything that can create division. These kinds of divisions were there in Corinth.

Such Divisions Being Condemned
by the Apostle's Teaching

Such divisions were condemned by the apostle's teaching. Paul said that those who make divisions are fleshly and walk according to the manner of man (1 Cor. 3:3-4). In 1 Corinthians 1:13 Paul said, "Is Christ divided? Was Paul crucified for you? Or were you baptized into the name of Paul?" The answer to all of these questions is "no." Christ, of course, is not divided. This unique and undivided Christ, taken as the unique center among all the believers, should be the termination of all divisions.

The Corinthians were also puffed up on behalf of one, against the other (1 Cor. 4:6). Paul and Apollos were simply ministers of Christ who should not have been appraised beyond what they were. Otherwise, their appraisers, like the fleshly Corinthians, might be puffed up on behalf of one, against the other. When we say that one brother is better than another brother, this can create division.

Such Divisive Ones Coming Together to Take the Lord's Table Not for the Better (Not for Profit) but for the Worse (for Loss)

When divisive ones come together to take the Lord's table, it is not for the better, not for profit, but for the worse, for loss (1 Cor. 11:17). How we come to the Lord's table is very important. We must have the assurance that we do not have any divisive thoughts or considerations about the saints. To come to the Lord's table in a divisive way will cause us to suffer loss.

Those who partake of the table in an unworthy manner fail to discern the bread as a symbol of the Lord's physical body that needs to be regarded by them. The bread on the table should also be discerned as a symbol of the Lord's mystical Body that requires us to keep the oneness of the Body of Christ. The denominations have their communion, their table, with the bread. But their bread does not signify the whole Body. It only signifies a part. That bread signifies division, so we cannot partake of it.

When we participate in the Lord's table, we must discern whether the bread on the table signifies the one Body of Christ or any division of man (any denomination). In discerning the Body of Christ, we should not partake of the bread in any division or with any divisive spirit. Otherwise, we will eat judgment to ourselves (1 Cor. 11:29). Paul said that because of this many among the Corinthians were weak and sick physically, and even a number were sleeping (v. 30). Here sleeping means that they had died (1 Thes. 4:13-16). First, they were disciplined to be weak physically. Then since they would not repent of their offense, they were further disciplined and became sick. Because they still would not repent, the Lord judged them by death. This shows that we have to be careful in coming to the Lord's table. When we come to the Lord's table, we have to discern the bread. It first signifies the physical body of Christ He gave for us on the cross. We should not consider this bread in a common way. We should also consider that this bread signifies Christ's mystical Body, which comprises all the believers in the whole universe. We do not take a divisive bread, but we take a bread of oneness. If we take divisive bread, we eat to our own judgment, to our own condemnation.

Parties of Division Manifesting
Those in the Church Life Who Are Approved

Parties of division manifest those in the church life who are approved (1 Cor. 11:19). Parties in the church are useful for manifesting the approved ones, who are not divisive. We need to be ones who are approved by God. If we are approved by God, we will not be divisive.

Having the Same Care for All the Members
to Avoid Division in the Body

We should have the same care for all the members to avoid division in the Body (1 Cor. 12:25). Philippians 2:2 says that we should have the same love toward all the saints. We may be loving one another with different levels of love. We may love one brother on the highest level and another one on the lowest level. In other words, we love certain brothers more than other brothers. This causes division.

In the church life, we may love the excellent, marvelous members, and look down on other members. However, the same care should be given to all the different members. A difference in care causes division. First Corinthians 12 says that those members of the Body which we consider to be less honorable, these we should clothe with more abundant honor. If a member is not so comely, we should bestow more honor to him to make him more comely (vv. 23-24). This is to balance the love and to balance the honor in the Body in order to avoid division. We should love everyone on the same level, trying to avoid division in every way.

No Base, No Reason, No Excuse, No Justification, and No Vindication for Any Kind of Division

There is no base, no reason, no excuse, no justification, and no vindication for any kind of division. Regardless of what the reason is for division, that is not a reason in the eyes of God. If we think that there is something wrong with the elders or the other saints, we should not gossip about them. We should always go to the Lord. If we go to the Lord, the Lord will impress us to pray for them. If there is something wrong, we should tell the Lord Jesus. He is the only One who can heal the situation. We also should check with ourselves whether or not we are better than they are. Are we better than the elders whom we are criticizing? If we get into the Lord's presence, we will realize that we are worse. The Lord will help us to realize that we need to be adjusted in many ways. This is the way to keep the oneness.

Always Remember:
There is No Way for the Members
of the Body of Christ to be Legitimately Divided
in the Body of Christ

We must always remember that there is no way for the members of the Body of Christ to be legitimately divided in the Body of Christ. In other words, no division is legitimate, and no division is justified, regardless of how strong our reason is.

All Problems Can and Should Be Solved
through Proper and Adequate Fellowship
by Praying Together Sincerely and Thoroughly

All problems can and should be solved through proper and adequate fellowship by praying together sincerely and thoroughly. Any question and any problem can be solved by fellowship. Acts 15 speaks of how the trouble concerning circumcision came from Jerusalem to Antioch. That stirred up a big turmoil in the church at Antioch. Paul and Barnabas, however, did not say, "This is something from Jerusalem. Let Jerusalem take care of this. We will tell these people to go back to Jerusalem. Antioch is our territory. It is in our jurisdiction." That is not the right way. Instead, Paul and Barnabas went from Antioch to Jerusalem to fellowship with the apostles and elders there (vv. 1-2). They all came together to have a thorough fellowship. By this kind of adequate and thorough fellowship, they arrived at a conclusion by the leading and guidance of the Spirit. Thus, they solved the problem.

Today we should be the same, but those who have been dissenting among us did not take this way. In recent years there have been some turmoils among us. When the dissenting ones came to me, a proposal was made to invite all the leading co-workers and the leading elders throughout the globe to come together. We would all come together to pray thoroughly, and then we would open up the holy Word to study and fellowship about all the concerns. They told me that they would agree on a date which would be acceptable for everyone to come together, and then they would let me know. Eventually, however, this never took place. That means they rejected the proper way to have fellowship. Thus far, none of the dissenting ones have come to me with a spirit of fellowship to fellowship about their problems. We all have to learn that if we see something that we cannot tolerate, the best way is to have fellowship with the concerned ones and with some experienced ones. By praying together to search the Word, we can solve every problem.

If we all hold to the unique faith, there should be no problem among us that cannot be solved. We all believe that God is triune and that the Bible is God's Word. We also believe that Christ is God becoming a man to be our Savior. He died on the cross for our sins and He resurrected physically, psychologically, and spiritually. Today He is our Savior and our life, and we are the children of the Triune God. As long as we believe in the contents of the faith, we should not contend for anything else. We do not need to argue with one another. Instead, we need to fellowship by praying together.

None of us should make an issue over the practice of

the new way versus the old way, because these ways are not our faith. Surely there is nothing wrong with preaching the gospel by visiting and contacting people. We do not necessarily need to go out to knock on people's doors to preach the gospel. Calling people on the phone, writing letters, sending booklets, and any other kind of contact with people is a kind of "knocking on doors." In order to keep the oneness, we need to remain in our spirit so that we can be kept in fellowship with the Lord. Then if there are problems, we can fellowship with those who are concerned. Based upon our fellowship with the Lord, with much prayer, we can get everything solved.

We should fellowship by seeking the Lord's solution with an open spirit, a pure heart, a lowly mind, and a meek attitude (Eph. 4:2). We should not be proud. Also, we should fellowship according to the teaching of the Scriptures properly interpreted, not understood by taking them out of context. Some may justify what they are doing by claiming that it is according to the Scriptures. However, it is according to the Scriptures by their wrong interpretation, by their twisting, and by their taking certain verses out of context.

Our fellowship to solve any problem should be without self-interest. The entire pursuit should be for the Lord's glory and for the benefit of the Lord's recovery. To solve any problem in fellowship, no parties or divisions should be formed for backing in partiality, threatening, and/or challenging others. If we would practice all these items, we surely can have every problem solved in fellowship. This is the best remedy to heal any disease of division.

Dealing with Divisive Members

There may be some divisive members among us. Paul referred to these ones in Romans 16:17, which says, "Now I exhort you, brothers, to mark those who make divisions and causes of stumbling contrary to the teaching which you have learned, and turn away from them." Some make division purposely. We have to turn away from these division-makers. Titus 3:10 says that we must reject the factious, sectarian, members. Some members are very factious, very sectarian, very divisive, and their purpose in contacting others is to cause division. There are some like this today who have the intention of remaining among us to spread their poison. No doubt, they are division-makers, and they are factious, sectarian. Since they are division-makers, we have to turn away from them. Since they are still factious after being admonished again and again, we have to reject them.

This is according to the practice of the quarantining of the lepers in typology (Lev. 13:45-46; Num. 12:10-15). When Moses' sister, Miriam, rebelled, God punished her with leprosy. Then she was quarantined. To be quarantined is to be put aside for the profit of the whole congregation. This is because certain diseases are very contagious. If a person is sick with a highly contagious disease, he is quarantined, separated even from his family members, until he is healed. This is for the protection of the entire family. The Scriptures charge us in the same way. Anyone who is spiritually sick of the disease of division, having become a divisive person, must be quarantined. Division is very contagious, so the church has to learn to quarantine the divisive ones. According to the apostle's teaching, we must either turn ourselves away from them or reject them. This protects the entire church so that the church can remain in a safeguarded situation.

I hope that the Holy Spirit will continue to speak to us through this fellowship. If we will spend the time to pray over this fellowship, we will see more light. All the local churches need to be kept in the oneness of the Body of Christ. The seven lampstands in Revelation, typifying the seven local churches, are all identical (1:12). They are all one in the Triune God. We need to be diligent to keep the oneness of the Body of Christ so that the Lord will have a way to accomplish His divine purpose according to His divine economy.

ABOUT THE AUTHOR

Witness Lee was born in 1905 in northern China and raised in a Christian family. At age nineteen he was fully captured for Christ and immediately consecrated himself to preach the gospel for the rest of his life. Early in his service, he met Watchman Nee, a renowned preacher, teacher, and writer. Witness Lee labored together with Watchman Nee under his direction. In 1934 Watchman Nee entrusted Witness Lee with the responsibility for his publication operation, called the Shanghai Gospel Book Room.

Prior to the Communist takeover in 1949, Witness Lee was sent by Watchman Nee and his other co-workers to Taiwan to ensure that the things delivered to them by the Lord would not be lost. Watchman Nee instructed Witness Lee to continue the former's publishing operation abroad as the Taiwan Gospel Book Room, which has been publicly recognized as the publisher of Watchman Nee's works outside China. Witness Lee's work in Taiwan manifested the Lord's abundant blessing. From a mere three hundred fifty believers, newly fled from the mainland, the churches in Taiwan grew to twenty thousand believers in five years.

In 1962 Witness Lee felt led of the Lord to move to the United States, and he began to minister in Los Angeles in December of that year. During his thirty-five years of service throughout the United States, he ministered in weekly meetings, weekend conferences, and weeklong trainings, delivering several thousand spoken messages. His speaking has since been published, and many of his books have been translated into numerous languages. He gave his last public conference in February 1997 at the age of ninety-one and went to be with the Lord, whom he loved and served, on June 9, 1997. Witness Lee leaves behind a prolific presentation of the truth in the Bible. His major work, *Life-study of the Bible,* the fruit of his labor from 1974 to 1995, comprises over twenty-five thousand pages of commentary on every book of the Bible from the perspective of the believers' enjoyment and experience of God's divine life in Christ through the Holy Spirit. In addition, *The Collected Works of Witness Lee* contains over one hundred thirty volumes (over seventy-five thousand pages) of his other ministry from 1932 to 1997. Witness Lee was also the chief editor of a new translation of the New Testament into Chinese called the Recovery Version, and he directed the translation of the English New Testament Recovery Version. The Recovery Version also appears in over twenty-five other languages. In the Recovery Version he provided an extensive body of footnotes, outlines, and spiritual cross references. A radio broadcast of his messages can be heard on Christian radio stations in the United States and Europe. In 1965 Witness Lee founded Living Stream Ministry, a non-profit corporation, located in Anaheim, California, which publishes his and Watchman Nee's ministry.

Witness Lee's ministry emphasizes the experience of Christ as life and the practical oneness of the believers as the Body of Christ. Stressing the importance of attending to both of these matters, he led the churches under his care to grow in Christian life and function. He was unbending in his conviction that God's goal is not narrow sectarianism but the universal Body of Christ. In time, believers everywhere began to meet simply as the church in their localities in response to this conviction. Through his ministry hundreds of local churches have been raised up throughout the earth.